The Magog Invasion

By
Chuck Missler

Contents

FORWARD
by HAL LINDSEY

I have know Chuck Missler as a close friend for almost twenty five years. He has the most extraordinary background of any Bible teacher I've ever known.

He was a honors graduate of the U.S. Naval Academy. He is a pioneer in computer technologies in many fields. He has participated in the development of some of the most exotic top secret military systems, including the stealth bomber and anti-submarine warfare.

He has served on projects for a former Chairman of Joint Chief of Staff, a former Chief of Naval Operations, a former Secretary of the Treasury. Chuck is familiar with many weapons which are still top secret.

Mr. Missler has organized joint ventures in high technology in the former Soviet Union, present Russia, Central Asia, North Africa, Europe and the Middle East. Some of these brought him into confrontation with the dreaded KGB. He is familiar with the workings of many of the world's top intelligence organizations.

I bring these things to your attention in order to point out that Mr. Missler is uniquely prepared to comment on the extremely important prophecy which is analyzed in this book.

Although Mr. Missler's high intelligence, education and experiences are important, they are overshadowed by his spiritual gifts of knowledge and teaching. Mr. Missler taught the Bible as a hobby for more than twenty years. But because of an extraordinary working of God in his life, he made his hobby his vocation. He quit a very successful business career in order to go into a full time study and exposition of the Bible.

Ezekiel, chapters 38 and 39, in my opinion give one of the most important prophecies of the Bible for our particular time in history. Chuck Missler has done a brilliant and inspired job of bringing new insight and documentation to this critical prophecy. Everyone should read his book, even if one does not agree with it.

I believe this book is destined to become a classic on the interpretation of Russia's fateful role in the most catastrophic war of all times.

Dedication

This book is dedicated to the loneliest people in the world: to those foreign service operatives who, because of the widespread corruption in the highest places, now discover that their leaders, and the institutions to which they have dedicated themselves to, are no longer committed to the same goals and objectives that once made public service a noble calling, and also now find that their leaders are no longer able to protect them.

This effort is especially dedicated to one who gave his life so that you and I could be truly free. (He will be specifically highlighted later in the book).

Acknowledgements

The sources and assistance for a project of this kind exceed our ability to be exhaustive. Furthermore, our diligence must be tempered with discretion. Surely our most valuable sources are ones which, of necessity, prefer (or insist) to remain anonymous. Our friends in the intelligence community, our many friends in Russia and Israel who have guided us and patiently tutored us over the years cannot begin to be listed here.

Among our scholastic debts, none are greater than those to Dr. Edwin Yamauchi and his many fine works. While greatly benefiting from his work and citations, the conclusions and mistakes are entirely our own.

Clearly, my deepest personal gratitude is due to my friend for over two decades, my personal tutor and mentor, and the one who personally recruited me into the full time ministry, Hal Lindsey. My personal intimacy with Hal Lindsey, Chuck Smith, and the late Dr. Walter Martin has given me a unique legacy . It is my earnest prayer that my efforts in my remaining years will yield fruit to their account. It was from a joint project with Hal that he encouraged me to compile our notes into this book.

To our friends in Russia and the Middle East, I can only hope that the turmoil of the coming years will somehow allow them personal safety.

To our friends in Israel, I pray that they discover their true Messiah and that He soon will bring them the peace that He has faithfully promised.

Chuck Missler
Coeur d'Alene, Idaho

Introduction

We are in possession of an astonishing message of extraterrestrial origin which should affect our national security as well as our personal agenda.

Chapter 1:

The Nature of Time

People like us, who believe in physics, know that the distinction between past, present, and the future is only a stubbornly persistent illusion.

-- Albert Einstein

This is, indeed, a strange book.

It explores a forthcoming climactic battle--the classic invasion of "Gog and Magog." This fabled confrontation has been the subject of speculations, conjectures and contentions ever since it was first predicted through the Prophet Ezekiel several thousand years ago. The more one knows about the details of this ancient text, and the more one is aware of the current intelligence picture of the Middle East, the more it appears that this astonishing event is about to take place.

And it will directly impact each of us. The preparations are already underway. As events continue to draw toward this dramatic confrontation, the implications for all of us are staggering. The advent of a nuclear war is terrifying, especially since it is unlikely to be confined only to the remote Middle East.

The recognition that we are, indeed, plunging into a period of history that has been pre-written in the classic pages of the Biblical record shatters the comfort of our preconceptions about time, our universe, and our physical reality.

The very premise that the Bible predicts certain portions of history, *in advance*, is manifestly a preposterous idea. It understandably strikes many people as the domain of crackpots and kooks.

Is it possible that the Bible really predicts world events *before they happen*? Is it really possible that the future can be known in advance?

We live in an age when the very nature of time is just beginning to be understood. The concepts of time warps, time travel, and the like, are not just the plaything of fiction writers, but now are the serious study of particle physicists, cosmologists, and other scientists. So before we address the specific example of this famous passage in the Bible, let us shed the baggage of some misconceptions which may hinder our understanding.

The Nature of Time

While philosophers throughout history have debated almost every idea under the sun since the world began, the one thing that they all have presumed--from the beginning--is that time is *linear* and *absolute*. Most of us assume that a minute a thousand years ago is the same as a minute today, and that we live in a dimension in which time inexorably rolls onward, yet is totally intractable to any attempt to glimpse ahead. We move forward and can look back; but we can't look ahead or move back. (Does anyone "remember" tomorrow?) Traversing the dimension of time remains the realm of fiction writers--and, apparently, a few strange experiments of the particle physicists.[1]

This linear view is also exemplified by our frequent resort

to "time lines." When we were in school, our teachers would draw a line on the blackboard. The left end of the line might represent the beginning of something--the birth of a person, or the founding of a nation, or an era. The right end of the line would demark the termination of that subject--the death of a person or the ending of an era.

Beginning   End
                              (Now)
_____

Therefore, when we encounter the concept of "eternity" we tend to view it as a *line of infinite length*--from "infinity" on the left and continuing toward "infinity" on the right. When we think of God, we naturally assume that He is someone "with lots of time."

But that view suffers from misconceptions based upon an obsolete physics. Today we owe a great debt to the insights of Dr. Albert Einstein.

A Geometry Lesson

How many degrees are there in a triangle? 180 is the expected answer. Every school boy knows that the sum of the angles in a triangle add up to 180°.

But suppose I take a transit and lay out a very *large* triangle, and discover that the three angles add up to *more than* 180°, say, 200°? What would you conclude?

That I made a mistake? Not necessarily. I may simply have encountered the *curvature* of the earth.

The assumptions that we all have grown accustomed to are from *plane* geometry--a geometry limited to two dimensions. If we take a course in navigation we encounter *spherical* trigonometry, where triangles can have 90° in *each* corner!

It was this type of insight that led Dr. Albert Einstein, in considering the nature of our physical universe, to realize that space is "curved." We live in more than just three dimensions, and time itself is that *fourth* physical dimension. This led to his famous Theory of Relativity--and the discovery that time itself is also part of our *physical* reality.

The Dimensions of Reality

We now realize that we live in (at least) a four-dimensional space, not just of three spatial dimensions of length, width and height, but also with an additional physical dimension of time.[2] Time is now known to be a *physical* property-- and it varies with mass, acceleration and gravity.

A time measurement device in a weaker gravitational field runs faster than one in a stronger field. Near the surface of the Earth the frequency of an atomic clock increases about one part in 10^{16} per meter, and, thus, a clock 100 meters higher than a reference clock will have a frequency greater by one part in 10^{14}.

Clocks carried eastward around the world in an airplane will differ (very slightly) from a clock at rest on the Earth, or one carried westward, since they are in rotation at different speeds about the center of the Earth and there is also a difference in gravitational potential.

In 1971, in experiments with atomic clocks by the U. S. Naval Observatory, atomic clocks were actually sent around the world in airplanes, one eastward and one westward. The eastward flying clock *lost* 0.06 microsecond with respect to one at rest, and the westward one *gained* 0.27 microsecond, confirming the predicted relativistic effects.

Who Cares?

I once served on the board of directors of a company which was in the process of acquiring a company which specialized in making cesium clocks. I remember when the president proudly announced that their key product was an atomic clock accurate to within one second in 100,000 years. I couldn't resist asking two questions: "How do you know?" And, "Who cares?"

It turns out that the accuracy of such a device can be predicted from the molecular behavior. And, furthermore, the accuracy of time measurement is a critical factor in the precision of navigation. The precision of their unique product now makes the Global Positioning Satellite navigation system possible.

The Twin Astronauts

Most discussions of the physics of time will also mention the interesting case of two hypothetical astronauts born at the same instant. One remains on the Earth; the other is sent on a space mission to the nearest star, Alpha Centauri, about 4 1/2 light years distant. If his vehicle travels at a speed of half the velocity of light, when our traveler returns to the Earth he will be more than *two years younger* than his twin brother! This example is often used to describe the *dilation* of time.

Our Common Misconception

Is God subject to gravity? Is He subject to the constraints of mass or acceleration? Hardly.

God is not someone "who has lots of time"; He is *outside* the domain of time altogether. That is what Isaiah means when he says, "It is He who inhabits eternity."[3]

Since God has the technology to create us in the first place, He certainly has the technology to get a message to us. But how does He *authenticate* His message? How does He assure us that the message is really from Him and not a fraud or a contrivance?

One way is to demonstrate that the message has its source from outside our time domain. God declares, "I alone know the end from the beginning."[4] His message includes history written in advance. We call this "prophecy."

An illustrative example is that of a parade. We sit on the curb, and observe the many bands, marching units, floats, and other elements coming around the corner and passing in front of us. The parade is--to us--clearly a *sequence* of events.

However, to someone who is *outside the plane of the parade's existence*--say, in a helicopter above the city--the beginning and the end are *simultaneously* in view. (It is amazing how many theological paradoxes evaporate when one recognizes the physical limitations of our dimension of time.)

A Message of Extraterrestrial Origin

We are in possession of a collection of 66 books we call The Bible, written by 40 authors, over the span of thousands of years, which we now discover is an *integrated* message from *outside of* our time domain. It repeatedly authenticates its uniqueness by describing history *before* it happens. And this discovery totally alters our concept of reality.[5]

There are numerous publications which document the many amazing examples of Biblical predictions which have been fulfilled in history.[6] However, our primary interests in this particular review are some events on our own immediate horizon. In fact, you and I are presently being plunged into a period of time about which the Bible says more *than any other period of time in history*--including the time when Jesus walked the shores of the Sea of Galilee and climbed the mountains of Judea.

So fasten your seat belts!

Why this Passage?

Among those who are familiar with Biblical prophecies, the passage in Ezekiel 38 (and 39) is very well known. This passage emerges quickly in any serious discussion of Bible prophecy for two principal reasons:

1) It is the occasion in which God dramatically intervenes in history to thwart an impending invasion of Israel.

2) Although penned more than 2,500 years ago, this unique event appears to describe the use of nuclear weapons.

Despite the popularity of this passage among "prophecy buffs," there remains a great deal of confusion and controversy over this well-known passage. However, the more you know about the details of this passage, and the more familiar you are about the current intelligence picture of the Middle East, the more it appears that this dramatic event *could* happen at any time.

In fact, this climactic battle now appears ready to begin at any moment.

In order to appreciate the implications of this critical passage of Scripture, it is essential to first identify the key players: who are *Gog and Magog?* Who are their allies?

While the identities of these peoples have been the subject of much controversy, fortunately, both ancient records and recent discoveries clearly identify the major players. By understanding who the players are, and then carefully observing the current world scene, you can determine for yourself the significance of the climactic events which are about to unfold.

It is, indeed, time to do our homework.

Endnotes:

1. There are examples in particle physics where a positron is understood to be an electron in a time reversal. See *Beyond Perception*, Koinonia House.

2. The ancient Hebrew scholar Nachmonides, writing in the 12th century, concluded from his studies of Genesis that the universe had 10 dimensions--only four are knowable, with six are beyond our knowing. It is interesting that particle physicists today have concluded that we live in 10 dimensions: 3 spatial dimensions and time are directly measureable. The remaining 6 are "curled" in less than 10^{-33} cm. and are only inferable by indirect means. (See *Beyond Perception*, Koinonia House.)

3. Isaiah 57:15.

4. Isaiah 46:10.

5. This is explored in the briefing packages, *The E.T. Scenario*, and *Beyond Time and Space*, Koinonia House.

    Koinonia House publishes briefing packages, each consisiting of two audio tape cassettes (each usually 90 mintes), and accompanied with study notes which include diagrams, references, etc.for further study of various Biblically relevant topics. These will be highlighted in the notes where appropriate.

6. See the briefing packages, *The Footprints of the Messiah*, and others from Koinonia House.

Chapter 2:

The Magog Identity

And the word of the LORD came unto me, saying,

Son of man, set thy face against Gog, the land of Magog, the chief prince of Meshech and Tubal, and prophesy against him,

. . .And I will turn thee back, and put hooks into thy jaws, and I will bring thee forth, and all thine army, horses and horse-men, all of them clothed with all sorts of armour, even a great company with bucklers and shields, all of them handling swords:

Ezekiel 38: 1-4

So begins this classic passage in which Gog and Magog, and their allies, are drawn into an invasion of Israel, only to have the God of Israel use the occasion to show Himself strong by intervening on behalf of His people by destroying the invading forces.

The Identities

To understand this passage, it is essential to first determine who the players really are. Despite the many controversies, these participants are surprisingly well identified. Just who are the people represented here by these ancient tribal names?

Why Such Weird Names?

It may seem strange that the Biblical prophets always seem to refer to various peoples by such strange ancient tribal names. Why do they?

It's our own fault! We always keep changing the names of things. There once was a city known as Petrograd. For many years it was known as St. Petersburg. Then it was changed to Leningrad. Now it is St. Petersburg again. What will it be named a few years from now?

(My friends in Russia say that, in Russia, even the *past* is uncertain!)

The capital of the old world, Byzantium, was renamed Constantinople. Now that city is known as Istanbul.

This occurs even in our own country. How many of you remember "Cape Canaveral?" Then it became Cape Kennedy. (It may have come dangerously close to being called "Cape Hillary!")

But we do not change the name of our *ancestors*! So, if you were the prophet Isaiah, and were called upon to speak of the Persians over a century *before* they emerged as an empire, how would you refer to them? You would speak of them as the descendants of Elam, the forebears of the Persians.[1]

The Table of Nations

Did you realize that you and I are related?

All of us are descendants, not only from Adam, but from Noah. Noah and his three sons repopulated the entire Earth after the flood. Thus, we are all descendants of Noah's three sons: Ham, Shem, and Japheth. We are all relatives. (Perhaps that's why we don't get along any better!)

The genealogical records of Noah and his three sons are listed in Genesis chapter 10, and the 70 original tribal groups described there are often called, by Biblical scholars, *The Table of Nations*. The diligent student needs to be familiar with these names. (A good study Bible, Bible Handbook, Dictionary, or Bible Encyclopedia can be helpful.)

Specifically, to understand the prophecies of Ezekiel 38 and 39, we need some background on Magog, and his allies. Fortunately, the identity of these ancient tribes is now relatively well understood and numerous sources and recent archaeological discoveries have clearly confirmed this identification.

Magog Identity

Magog was one of the sons of Japheth[2]. There have been controversies with respect to Gog and Magog,[3] but the traditional experts and most reputable sources have always identified Magog as referring to the ancient peoples known as the Scythians.[4]

The Ancient Historians

One of the earliest references to Magog was by Hesiod, "the father of Greek didactic poetry," who identified Magog with the Scythians and southern Russia in the 7th century B.C.[5] Hesiod was, in effect, a contemporary of Ezekiel.

Another of the major sources on the ancient history of the Middle East is, of course, Josephus Flavius, who clearly identified Magog:

> *"Magog founded the Magogians, thus named after him, but who were by the Greeks are called Scythians."*[6]

Another 1st century writer was Philo[7] who also identified Magog with southern Russia.

But most of our information comes to us from Herodotus

who wrote extensively in the 5th century B.C.

The Father of History

Herodotus of Halicarnassus is known as the "Father of History." He wrote the earliest important historical narrative, in which he described the background and the course of the great war between the Greeks and the Persians in the 5th century B.C. After the Peace of Callias (449 B.C.), Herodotus was free to travel throughout the Near East, visiting Egypt and Mesopotamia. Possessed of an omnivorous curiosity, Herodotus was the tourist par excellence.

Many scholars have, from time to time, been critical of Herodotus' accounts,[8] but numerous archeological discoveries have clearly confirmed Herodotus' reports in general, and his Scythian accounts in particular.[9]

In the 7th century B.C. the Greeks renewed their efforts at colonization. The Ionian city of Miletus took the lead in the northeast, establishing nearly a hundred colonies around the shore of the Black Sea.[10] One of the most important of these colonies was Olbia, founded in 645 B.C. at the mouth of the Bug and Dnieper Rivers.[11] It was probably from this "port of Borysthenites" [12] that the Greek historian obtained most of his information about the Scythians, who lived in close proximity.[13] In his significant study of Herodotus' "Scythia" (i.e., book 4), the Soviet scholar, B. A. Rybakov, concludes that Herodotus probably made a complete circuit of the Black Sea in order to obtain further data.[14]

Herodotus recounts many bizarre and savage practices of the descendants of Magog known as the Scythians: they drank the blood of the first enemy killed;[15] they carried the heads of their victims to their chiefs;[16] they scalped their enemies and used these scalps as "napkins"; [17]they used the skins of their victims to cover their quivers;[18] they drank from the skulls of their victims;[19] they practiced blood brotherhood by drinking each other's blood mixed with wine.[20] The Scythians "bathed" in the vapor from heated hemp seeds.[21] When their king died, they sacrificed one of his concubines and several servants.[22] After a year, they commemorated his death by sacrificing fifty servants and fifty horses.[23]

Rough bunch, these Scyths.

The tortuous path from the horseback archery of the early Scyths to the nuclear missiles of the Russian Federation includes many centuries of turbulent history. The various descendants of Magog terrorized the southern steppes of Russia from the Ukraine to the Great Wall of China. Our next section will provide a summary of this colorful--and violent--path through the "steppes of history."

Endnotes:

1.   Isaiah 11:11; 21:2; 22:6.

2.   Genesis 10:2; I Chronicles 1:5

3.   G. Husing, "Gugu," *Orientalistische Literaturzeitung* 18, 1915,pp. 299-302; J. L
      Myres, "Gog and the Danger from the North in Ezekiel," *Quarterly Statement,
      Palestine Exploration Fund, 1932,* 213-219; J. G. Alders, *Gog en Magog in
      Ezekiel,* J. H Kok, Kamapen, 1951; M. C. Astour, "Ezekiel's Prophecy of Gog and
      the Cutherean Legend of Naram-Sin", *Journal of Biblical Literature,* 95.4, 1976, pp.
      567-579.

4.   Keil, C.F., and Delitzsch, F., *Biblical Commentary on the Prophecies of Ezekiel,* T.
      and T. Clark, Edinburgh, 1891, vol 2, p. 157; Gesenius, Wilhelm, *A Hebrew and
      English Lexicon of the Old Testament,* Crocker and Brewster, Boston, 1872, pp.
      534, 626, 955, 1121; Scofield, C.I., ed., *The Scofield Reference Bible,* Oxford
      University, 1917, p. 883; *The New Scofield Reference Bible*, English, E.S., 1967, p.
      881.

5.   F. W. Gingrich and Frederich Danker, *A Greek-English Lexicon of the New
      Testament and other Early Christian Literature,*   University of Chicago Press,
      Chicago and London, 1957.

6.   Josephus, *Antiquities,* 1.123; Jerome, *Commentary on Ezekiel* 38:2.

7.   F. H. Colson, G.H. Whitaker, and Ralph Marcus, *Philo,* Loeb Classical Library,
      London, 1929-1953.

8.   K. W. Nitzsch (1872); A. H. Sayce (1883); H. Delbruck (1887); A.T. Olmstead
      (1916);Ph. E. Legrand, "De la 'malignite d'Herodote," *Melanges Gustav Glotz,*
      Presses Universitaires de France, Paris, 1932, Vol 2, pp. 535-547; J. A. S. Evans,
      "Father of History or Father of Lies?" *Classical Journal* 64, 1968, pp. 11-17; F.
      Wilke, "Das Skythenproblem im Jeremiabuch," in *Alttestamentliche Studien fur R.
      Kittle,* J. C. Hinrichs, Leipzig, 1913, pp. 222-254.

9.   W. Spiegelberg, *The Credibility of Herodotus' Account of Egypt in the Light of the
      Egyptian Monuments,* Blackwell, Oxford, 1927; O. E. Ravn, *Herodotus'
      Description of Babylon,* A. Busck, Copenhagen, 1942.

10.   T. J. Dunbabin, *The Greeks and Their Eastern Neighbours,* Society for the
      Promotion of Hellenic Studies, London, 1959; J. M. Cook, *The Greeks in Ionia and
      the East,* Praeger, New York, 1963; John Boardsman, *The Greeks Overseas,* 2nd ed.,
      Thames and Hudson, London, 1980.

11.   R. Rice, *The Scythians,* 3rd ed., Praeger, New York, 1961, pp. 23, 49-54; T.
      Sulimirski, "Greek Colonization and the Early Iron Age East of the Volga," *Bulletin
      of the Institute of Archaeology,* London, 11, 1973, pp. 15-19; E.H. Minns, "Thirty

Years of Work at Olbia," *Journal of Hellenic Studies,* 65, 1945, pp. 109-112.

12. Herodotus 4.17.

13. W. W. How and J. Wells, *A Commentary on Herodotus,* Clarendon, Oxford, 1961, Vol 1, p. 308; A. de Selincourt, *The World of Herodotus,* Little, Brown, Boston, 1962, p. 239; B. N. Grakow, *Die Skythen,* Deutscher Verlag der Wissenschaften, Berlin, 1980, p. 9.

14. B.A. Rybakov, Геродотова Скифия (Herodotus's Scythia), Nauka, Moscow, 1979, p. 79.

15. Herodotus 4.64.

16. Rice, Scythians, p. 54, fig. 3 depicts a Scythian holding the head of his victim.

17. Herodotus 4.64.

18. *Ibid.,* 4.64.

19. *Ibid.,* 4.65.

20. *Ibid.,* 4.70.

21. *Ibid.,* 4.75.

22. *Ibid.,* 4.71.

23. *Ibid.,* 4.72.

The Steppes of History

A brief review of the history
of a violent and colorful people
who again will shape the
world's destiny.

Chapter 3:

Early Origins

History teaches us that man learns nothing from history.

Georg Wilhelm Friedrich Hegel

T he earliest origins of the area settled by the descendants of Magog, the extreme north and east, are clouded in the mists of antiquity and from the nomadic nature of the numerous and mobile empires and the winds of war that crisscrossed the sands of time. Only faint traces remain, but enough to establish the critical identities. Our indebtedness extends from writers predating Ezekiel to the energies of the Russian archaeologists in more recent years.

The Urartu

During the first half of the second millennium B.C., the Hurrians (who had come into the Near East from the north early in the third millennium B.C.) dominated most of Syria and northern Mesopotamia under the control of Mitannian over-lords. Around 1000 B.C., after the fall of the Mitannian state, a Hurrian tribe, called the Nairi, began to unite in northeastern Anatolia. In the ninth century B.C. these tribes created a new state in the region of Lake Van in present-day Turkey, which immediately became a competitor of Assyria. The Assyrians called this state *Urartu*. In Urartean inscriptions, the center of their territory was called the country of the Biainnili.

Monuments of the Assyrian king Shalmaneser III[1] includes written information about the Urarteans. From the first year of his reign, Shalmaneser led uninterrupted wars against his northern neighbors. These campaigns are described in his annals and depicted on the bronze gates of a temple at Balawat near Nineveh.[2]

Despite this opposition, the Urartean state quickly became powerful, and in the first half of the eighth century B.C. extended its rule over a wide area.

Having entered into an alliance with the small states in northern Syria, the Urarteans took possession of the lands down to the western bend of the Euphrates River, gaining control of a main route to the Mediterranean from the southern Caucasus. Simultaneously they began to subjugate the southern Caucasus itself, including the fertile valley of the middle Araxes River and the mountains of Armenia, rich in copper ore and in cattle. Overcoming the resistance of local chieftains, the Urarteans seized the land around Mount Ararat and Lake Sevan (the largest lake in Transcaucasia, in central Armenia), and established military and administrative centers there.

In 782 B.C. the Urartean king Argishti I founded Erebuni, a fortress on the northern edge of Araxes valley, where he settled 6,600 prisoners. Somewhat later he founded Argishtihinili ("built by King Argishti"), a large city on the banks of the Araxes River.

Assyria could not stand by indifferently as Urartu expanded and grew more powerful. During the reign of Argishti's son, Sarduri II (764-735 B.C.), the Assyrians undertook two campaigns against Urartu, in 743 and 735 B.C. In the second, they reached and besieged the Urartean capital of Tushpa.

Two groups are frequently referred to in Urartean and Assyrian texts: the Cimmerians and the Scythians. Both will figure prominently in subsequent identifications.

In the Assyrian royal archive, found in their capital of Nineveh, there is a dispatch from the crown prince Sennacherib[3] who reports that Cimmerian nomads were marching against Urartu. It describes how they had inflicted a defeat on the Urartean forces, and lists the names of the Urartean commanders who fell in battle.

Sargon, encouraged by this defeat to his archenemy, led an ambitious campaign against Urartu in 714 B.C. It ended in a complete victory for the Assyrians, which is described in a long text on a clay tablet found at Assur, while scenes from the campaign, such as plundering the Urartean temple in Musasir, southeast of Lake Van, are represented on the walls of the royal palace at Dur Sharrukin (Khorsabad).

Cimmerians

The Cimmerians are the oldest of the European tribes living north of the Black Sea and Danube, and whom we know by the name they used for themselves. The Cimmerian period in the history of southern Ukraine began in the late 11th century B.C.

The prehistory of the Cimmerians has also been subject of much controversy.[4] The Cimmerians were the first specialized horse-nomads to make their name in history.[5]

The earliest osteological evidence of the domestication of the horse occurs south of Kiev about 2500 B.C.[6] Earliest textual evidence for the use of horses comes from the Ur III period (21st century) of Mesopotamia.[7] The nomadic lifestyle, including mounted warriors, fully developed between the 10th and 8th centuries.[8] The casting details of the horse bridles--the bit, snaffle and small bells--suggest that they were used not only for saddle horses, but also for chariots.

We find the first mention of them in secular literature in *The Odyssey* and *The Iliad* of Homer (8th Century B.C.), and in Assyrian cuneiform texts from the 8th century B.C. (before Ezekiel), and, of course, in Herodotus (5th century B.C.). Herodotus indicates that the whole of the North Pontic steppe region, occupied in his time by the Scythians, belonged earlier to the Cimmerians.[9] Homer[10] associated the Cimmerians with a fogbound land, perhaps the Crimean peninsula on the north shore of the Black Sea. Some scholars derive the name of "Crimea" from the Cimmerians.[11]

The Cimmerians surged into Asia Minor in the 70's of the 7th century B.C. They annihilated the Phrygian kingdom after destroying and looting its capital, Gordium. In 652 B.C. they captured Sardis and plundered the Greek cities of the Aegean coast and Asia Minor. In the 30's of the 7th century, Cimmerian forces were checked and routed by the Assyrians who came to the aid of the Scythians. By the 6th century the name of the Cimmerians disappeared from the historical scene.

In the 5th Century, Herodotus[12] related that the Cimmerians were driven south over the Caucasus, probably through the central Dariel Pass, by the Scythians in a domino-like effect as the Scythians themselves were pushed westward by other tribes.

This can be correlated with Chinese records.[13]

The numerous references in the Talmud has left little doubt that these descendants of Gomer moved northward and established themselves in the Rhine and Danube valleys.[14]

The Cimmerians will be discussed further as the descendants of Gomer, which is one of the allies in the Magog invasion, reviewed in chapter 7.

The Scythians

In the 7th century B.C. a wave of Asiatic nomads, known in history as the Scythians, swept across the area, displacing the Cimmerians from the steppes of the Ukraine east of Dnieper River, who fled from them across the Caucasus.

According to Herodotus[15]:

"The Scythians pursued (the Cimmerians) with the Caucasus on their right till where they came into the Median land, turning inland on their way."

Most authorities believe that these Scythians came south through the Caucasus by way of the Derbent Pass along the west coast of the Caspian Sea.[16]

It is provocative that even the name "Caucasus" appears to have been derived from *Gog-hasan,* or "Gog's Fort."[17]

Archaelolgical evidence suggests that the Scythians infiltrated into the area of Transcaucasia (south of the Caucasus) even earlier than the 10th century B.C. It was probably in this area that they first developed their distinctive trilobate arrows.[18]

Assyrian texts mention the Scythians in the 8th century. A relief from the early 9th century, during the reign of Ashurnasirpal II (883-859 B.C.) portrays mounted Scythian bowmen, wearing pointed caps, soft top boots and trousers.[19]

Excavations in the Armenian and Azerbaijan republics document the Scythian presence in Transcaucasia, in particular, the fall of Karmir-Blur (ancient Teishebaini) founded by Rusa II in the mid-7th century.[20]

Other evidences of the Scythian penetration south are the presence of horse burials and equestrian equipment at Hasanlu[21] and Baba Jan.[22]

The first reference to the Ishkuza (the Assyrian name for the Scyths) is in texts from the reign of Sargon II (721-705 B.C.), but there are far fewer references to the Ishkuza than to the Gimmiraia in the Neo-Assyrian texts. The most important references come from the reign of Esarhaddon (680-669 B.C.).[23]

The hippomolgoi ("mare-milkers") mentioned in Homer's *Iliad*[24] were equestrian nomads of the northern steppes and several authorities identified these with the Scythians.[25]

[One of the delicacies I was presented with when I was being hosted by the Deputy Chairman of the Soviet Union, was fermented horse milk! These traditions may have a deep history, indeed.]

By far the most critical identification, for our purposes, are these people--identified by their contemporaries and other early historians as the descendants of Magog--and so they are the focus of our next chapter.

Endnotes:

1. Shalmaneser III (858-824 B.C.), son of Ashurnasirpal II, was the first Assyrian king to come into direct contact with Israel.

2. Encyclopedia Britannica, 10:692:1a.

3. Sennacherib, King of Assyria and Babylonia (705-681 B.C.). His seiges against Israel were unsuccessful due to Hezekiah's foresight in protecting his water supplies (2 Kings 20:20; 2 Chronicles 32:30), and the Angel of the Lord (2 Kings 19:35).

4. C. F. Lehmann-Haupt, "Zur Chronologie der Kimmeriereinfalle," *Klio* 17, 1921, pp.112-122; A. Baschunakoff, "Le probleme scythique et l'enigme cimmerienne," *Revue anthropologique* 92, 1932, pp.142-168; J. Harmatta, "Le probleme cimmerien," *Archaeologiai Ertesito*, ser. III, 7-9, 1946-1948, pp. 79-132; M. Gimbutas, *Prehistory of Eastern Europe,* Peabody Museum, Cambridge MA, 1956, pp. 80-92; T. Sulimirski, "The Cimmerian Problem," *Bulletin of Institute of Archaeology* 2, 1959, pp. 62-63; also, *Prehistoric Russia: An Outline,* Humanities Press, NY, 1970, pp. 395-397. R.S. Young, "The Nomadic Impact: Gordion," *Dark Ages and Nomads c. 1000 B.C.,* ed. M.J. Melink, Nederlands Histoisch-Archaeologisch Instituut, Istanbul, 1964, p. 56.

5. E. D. Phillips, "New Light on the Ancient History of the Eurasian Steppe," *American Journal of Archaeology* 61, 1957, p. 274.

6. J. F. Downs, "The Origin and Spread of Riding in the Near East and Central Asia," *American Anthropologist* 63, 1961, p. 1196.

7. P.R.S. Moorey, "Evidence for the History of Horse-Riding in Iraq before the Kassite Period," *Iraq* 32, 1970, pp. 36-50.

8. K. Jettmar, "Die Entstehung der Reiternomaden," *Saeculum* 17, 1966, p. 1-11.; E.D. Phillips, "New Light on the Ancient History of the Eurasian Steppe," *American Journal of Archaelogy,* 61, 1957.

9. Herodotus 4.11.

10. *Odyssey,* 11.13-19.

11. Strabo 7.4.3.

12. Herodotus 4.11-13.

13. T. Rice, *The Scythians,* 3rd ed., Praeger, NY, 1961, p. 43.

14. Targum Yonasan and the Midrash: identification with Germania.

15. Herodotus 4.12.

16. P. N. Tretiakov and A. L. Mongait, eds., *Contributions to the Ancient History of the USSR,* Peabody Museum, Cambridge MA, 1961, p. 60.

17. Dr. John Gill, *A Commentary on the Old Testament,* 1748.

18. T. Sulimirski, "Scythian Antiquities in Western Asia," *Artibus Asiae,* 17, 1954, p. 283.

19. T. Sulimirski, *Prehistoric Russia: An Outline,* Humanities Press, NY, 1970, p. 397. Y. Yadin, *The Art of Warfare in Biblical Lands,* Weidenfeld and Nicolson, London, 1963, p. 385-385.

20. B. Piotrovsky, *The Ancient Civilization of Urartu,* Cowles, NY, 1969, p. 25; [Piotrovsky excavated Karmir-Blur between 1929 and 1941 and since 1949 for the Armenian Academy of Sciences]; R. Rolle, "Urartu and die Reiternomaden,", *Saeculum* 28, 1977, p. 324.

21. R. H. Dyson, "Further Excavations at Tepe Hasanluy, Iran," *Archaeology,* 26, 1973, pp. 303-304; The Architecture of Hasanlyu," *American Journal of Archaeology,* 81, 1977, p. 548-552; R. Ghirshman, "Invasion des nomades," *Dark Ages and Nomads, c. 1000 B.C.,* ed. M. J. Mellink, Nederlands Historisch-Archaeologisch Instituut, Istanbul, 1964, p. 5.

22. C. Goff Meade, "Excavations at Baba Jan, 1967," *Iran* 7, 1969, pp. 123-126.

23. D.D. Luckenbill, ed. *Ancient Records of Assyria and Babylonia,* University of Chicago, 1927, vol 2, pp. 207, 213; R. C. Thomposon, *The Prisms of Esarhaddon and Ashurbanipal,* British Museum, London, 191, p. 19; A. Heidel, "A New Hexagonal Prism of Esarhaddon," *Sumer* 12, 1956, p. 17.

24. *Iliad,* 13.5.

25. B.N. Grakov, *Die Skythen,* Deutscher Verlag der Wissenschaften, Berlin, 1980, p. 4.

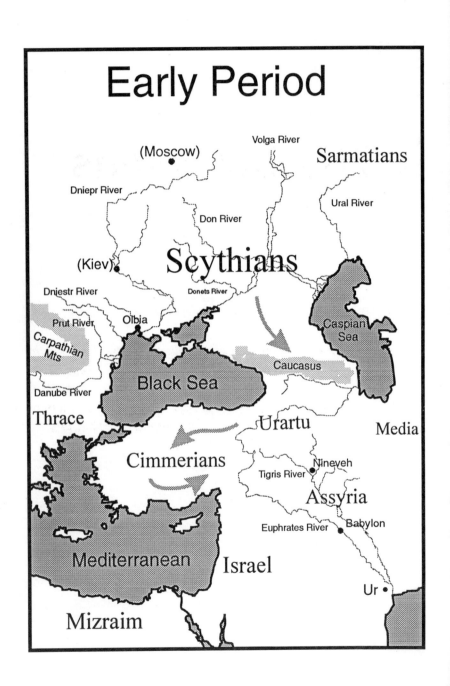

Chapter 4:

The Scythians

"No one confronting them can escape on foot, and if they wish not to be discovered it is impossible to engage with them. The reason is that they do not build towns or fortresses, but all of them are mounted archers and carry their homes with them... How can they fail to be invincible, and immune from attack?"

Herodotus, 5th century B.C.

"But even Scythians, who delight in murdering people and are little better than wild beasts, nevertheless think it their duty to uphold their national customs."

Josephus Flavius, 1st century A.D.

W e know the descendants of Magog by their Greek designation as the *Scythians*, (depicted in their legends as descending from *Scythes*, the youngest of the three sons of Heracles, from sleeping with a half viper and half woman).[1]

The name Scythian designates a number of nomadic tribes from the Russian steppes, one group of which invaded the Near East in the 8th and 7th centuries B.C. After being repulsed from Media, many of the later Scyths settled in the fertile area of the Ukraine north of the Black Sea. Other related tribes occupied the area to the east of the Caspian Sea.

Herodotus describes them living in *Scythia*, (i.e., the territory north of the Black Sea) and who spoke the Scythian language, which belonged to the Iranian family of the Indo-European languages.[2] The Ossetian dialect of central Caucasus appears to be a survival.[3]

The original area in which Iranian was spoken extended from the mid-Volga and the Don regions to the northern Urals and beyond. From here Iranian-speaking tribes colonized Media, Parthia, Persia, Central Asia and as far as the Chinese border.

Herodotus distinguishes three groups of Scyths in this area:

1)   The agricultural Scythians[4] who lived in the interior, northwest of the Crimea; [5]

2)   The nomadic Scythians[6] who lived to the east of the agricultural Scythians;

3)   The royal Scyths[7] who lived in the area directly to the north and to the east.

Herodotus also gives us detailed information on the neighboring tribes, the Alazones,[8] Callippidae,[9] Sauromatae or Sarmatians,[10] "Black Cloaks",[11] Agathyrsi,[12] Geloni,[13] Neuri,[14] Budini,[15] "Man-Eaters",[16] Thyssagetae[17] and the Iyrkae.[18]

Tombs that Tell Tales

The fact that the Scythian culture extended more than 2,000 miles east from the Ukraine was demonstrated by the sensational discovery of tombs in the Chilikta Valley of East Kazakhstan, published in Russian in 1965,

> "...prove that Scythian material culture had spread to the Mongolian border as early as the 6th century B.C."[19]

Countless Scythian burials, ranging from the 6th to the 2nd century, have been uncovered in the areas to the north and east of the Black Sea, in many cases beyond the limits of what Herodotus demarcated in his day as "Scythia" proper. Soviet scholars have, of course, worked broadly in this region.[20]

Fabulous gold treasures discovered in royal Scythian kurgans (barrows, or graves) aroused the attention of Europe in the 17th century and more than 20,000 gold objects fill the rooms of the Hermitage Museum in St. Petersburg.[21]

The most spectacular discovery of tombs which illuminate the account of the Scythians occurred at the eastern end of the Russian steppes, the famed frozen tombs of Pazyryk. These are located in the Altai Mountains of southern Siberia, just north of the westernmost boundary of the Mongolian People's Republic near the headwaters of the Ob River.

The Pazyryk tombs were first discovered by S. I. Rudenko in 1924. He conducted excavations there in 1929 and in 1947 through 1949. Though partial accounts appeared earlier,[22] a comprehensive treatment did not appear in English until 1970.[23]

Remarkable circumstances led to the preservation of otherwise perishable materials. The frozen conditions marvelously preserved textiles, remains of horses, human skin and hair, entrails, undigested food, etc., for more than 2,300 years!

In July 1995, Russian archaeologists found a 2,500 year old Scythian horseman under more than 7 feet of ice in Siberia near the Chinese and Mongolian borders. More than 6,500 feet above sea level, the Ukok Plateau is blanketed by a thick layer of rocks that keeps the ground frozen the year around. The horseman had been given his ceremonial burial in his fur coat and high leather boots, alongside his horse in a log-lined chamber in the Altai Mountains. He also had his ax, quiver, and dagger.[24] A year earlier, the Ukok Plateau yielded its first major mummy, a Scythian princess.

The Biological Structures Research Institute (which tends Lenin's preserved remains) has developed special technologies to deal with such finds, in support of the Russian Academy of Science's Institute of Archaeology and Ethnology in Novosibirsk.

The most significant archaeological site associated with the 7th century B.C. agricultural Scythians is Nemirov Gorodische, located halfway between Odessa and Kiev, excavated in 1946 through 1948 by M. Artamonov.[25]

More than 1,200 graves have been investigated by A. Leskov in the Crimean area between 1961 and 1972. Aerial surveys also have been employed.[26] Hundreds of Scythian graves of the 4th and 3rd centuries have been discovered since the 1930's by B. Grakow, A. Trenoschkin, and E. Tschernenko, in the Ukraine.

The Ziwiye Treasures

Herodotus indicates that the Scythians were active in Media southwest of Lake Urmia. It is also evident in the Assyrian texts that the Scythians were active directly south of the lake. A spectacular discovery of treasure at Ziwiye in this area now offers corroborative evidence of the Herodotus' accounts.

Ziwiye is 25 miles east of modern Sakkez[27] in Kurdistan in northwestern Iran. The name Ziwiye may preserve the Akkadian name Zibie (Izibie), a site attacked by Sargon II in 716 and by Ashurbanipal in about 665. A total of 341 objects was in the inventory: 43 in gold, 71 in silver, 103 in ivory, etc.[28]

A Scythian chief named Bartatua[29] demanded an Assyrian princess in marriage as the price for his allegiance. His son also fought for the Assyrians against the Cimmerians in Cappodocia in 654 B.C.[30] There is some evidence that the treasure may have belonged to the Scythian prince Madyes, whose father Bartatua had married Esarhaddon's daughter.[31]

According to Herodotus[32] the Median king Cyaxares II (625-585 B.C.) was attacked by a Scythian horde, led by Madyes, son of Bartatua. Herodotus further states[33]:

"The Scythains, as I have before shown, ruled the upper country of Asia for 28 years."

("Asia" seems to have originally referred to an area on the west coast of Turkey known in Hittite as Assuwa.[34] In New Testament times Asia designated the Roman province around Ephesus, and even the entire peninsula of Turkey in the phrase "Asia Minor."[35])

One of the many implications of the Soviet finds is the authentication of the reliability of Herodotus as a source of knowledge of the Scythians. The leading authorities on the Scythians, T. Rice, T. Sulimirski, and others, all regard Herodotus as thoroughly vindicated.[36]

The Agricultural Scythians

Archaeological research also shows that the areas settled by the agricultural tribes were highly developed both economically and culturally. Here there were hill forts and settlements in which were manufactured metal tools, weapons, and ornaments. There was an active trade with the Greek colonies and with their neighbors to the west.

The population between the Dnieper (which the Greeks called the Boristhenes) and Dniester was of "ploughmen-Scythians" who produced grain (cereals, millet, onions, garlic and lentils) for sale. These "ploughmen" Scythians were probably the proto-Slavs. (These will be reviewed in chapter 6.)

The Nomadic Scythians

East of these agricultural Scythians lived the nomadic Scythians, "the bravest and most numerous of the Scythians, who regard the other Scythians as their slaves."

The nomadic Scythians occupied the steppe region of modern Ukraine where they raised horses, sheep and other domestic animals. They migrated according to the season, looking for the most favorable pasture. "No one confronting them can escape on foot, and if they wish not to be discovered it is impossible to engage with them. The reason is that they do not build towns or fortresses, but all of them are mounted archers and carry their homes with them, living in their wagons, and gain their sustenance not from the plough but from raising domestic animals. How can they fail to be invincible, and immune from attack?"[37]

Scythian Horsemanship

The Scythians were among the most skilled horsemen ever known. It was their superb horsemanship, especially in their ability to shoot arrows while riding at a full gallop, even at enemies behind them, that gave the Scythians and their later imitators, the Parthians, a distinctive military advantage.[38]

Scythians rode without benefit of stirrups, which were probably invented by their eastern neighbors, the Sarmatians, who began to dominate the Ukraine from about A.D. 200.[39]

Scythians wore pointed hats, which were probably made of leather. For utility in riding, the Scythians may have "invented" trousers.[40] Their trousers and matching jackets were decorated with multihued dots, rosettes, or zigzags.[41] Tombs indicate that some of the Scythians adopted scale armor, which had long been in use in the Near East.[42]

Scythian Archery

The Scythians were among the earliest mounted archers in antiquity.[43] They were certainly among the most skilled, even able to fire backwards while riding at a gallop.[44] Such a skill is best learned from childhood.[45] According to Plato[46] the Scythians could shoot as easily with the left as with the right hand. Lucian[47] relates that while galloping they were able to hit a moving beast or bird.[48]

Though the Scythians had other weapons such as battle-axes, daggers, spears, and swords, they were most effective with the bow. They would advance quickly, fire their arrows, and retreat before their enemies could engage them. These hit-and-run tactics frustrated Darius when he invaded Thrace and Scythia[49] It was Alexander's genius that enabled him to lure the Scythians east of the Caspian Sea into a trap.[50]

The Scythians used short (40-43 inches) but powerful bows. Scyth bows were made up of three parts: (1) the inner face made of strips of horn, placed in (2) a groove of wood, and (3) the outer face of flexible sinew.[51] Scyth bows resembled a capital sigma ($\sum$), that is, they curved inwards in the center and outwards at the ends.[52] The completion of a proper Scythian bow may have required as much as five to ten years.[53]

The Scythians used a special combination of quiver and bow case called a *gorytus*. The lower portion held the bow, and the upper portion could hold as many as two to three hundred arrows.[54] The Scythians kept the gorytus at waist level on the left side to give them ready access to the arrows while they were riding. The gorytus was often highly decorated with leather and even with gold.

The Scythian arrow shafts were very light and relatively short--between 18 and 30 inches.[55] They were made either of reeds or of birch or yew twigs.[56] Distinctive socketed arrow-heads, especially adapted for light arrows, were developed by the Scythians early in the first millennium in Transcaucasia. They were of three types: (1) a trilobate (three bladed) type, (2) a pyramidal type, and (3) a leaf (two-bladed) type. They were small, about an inch in length, and cast in bronze rather than iron. Thousands of such arrowheads have been found in Scythia, that is, the region north of the Black Sea.[57]

The Scythians in Asia Minor

It was in the late 7th or early 6th century B.C. (during the rise of Babylon under Nebuchadnezzar and the time of Ezekiel) that the forest-steppe regions along the River Dnieper were incorporated into Scythia.

The Scythians held sway in Asia Minor for 28 years (652-625 B.C.), laying it waste by excessive tributes and plundering. This was brought to an end when Cyaxares and the Medes invited the greater number of them to a feast, made them exceedingly drunk, and slaughtered them[58].

"After suffering defeat, the Scythians returned to their own country[59]," the steppes of both the northern Caucasus and the Black Sea area. The northern Caucasus was the natural launching pad for raids into the Near East. Here the Scythians returned after their defeat, and became the dominant power in that area.

Herodotus relates how the Scythians, having returned from Asia, endured a great war in their homeland "no less than that with the Medes." Resisting the Scythians were the children born to their wives, who had been left behind during the raids, and slaves. "Having discovered the circumstances of their birth, they resolved to offer resistance to those returning from the country of the Medes." The Scythians ultimately prevailed, using horse whips rather than conventional weapons of spears and bows--thus psyching them into reacting as slaves rather than as peers.

According to Herodotus and archaeological evidence, the Scythians occupied territory from the Danube to the Don. The northern boundary extended beyond the latitude of Kiev. Near Olbia lived the Callipidae and Graeco-Scythians, and farther north, the Alazones.

Almost at the same time as the Scythians appeared in the Black Sea area, settlers arrived from Greece and Asia Minor (Ionia) to establish colonies on the Black Sea coast. The northern Black Sea became a melting pot of cultures, including the traditions of the Greeks, Scythians, and other peoples.

They founded colonial cities along the coast with attractive names, as Olbia (meaning "happy"), Theodosia and Panti-capaeum. The Greek settlers entered into close relations with their neighbors, the "barbarians" (which is what the Greeks called all non-Greeks). Herodotus visted Olbia in the 5th century and learned of their legends and customs.

The relations with the Greeks were peaceful, and regulated by agreements. The agricultural and nomadic Scythians coexisted in one state, but some of them regarded the rest as their slaves or tributaries.

Defense in Depth

One reason Herodotus gave so much detailed information about the Scythians was that he wanted to describe the people who had succeeded in defeating the Persian king Darius. This was a most important element in the history of Scythians, and the memory of it remained with them for many years.

In resisting the Persians, a provocative strategic tradition was born: *Defense in Depth*. This unique strategy also would characterize these descendants of Magog in more recent times against both Napoleon and Hitler.

Darius I crossed the Bosphorus and invaded Scythia. The Scythians, however, had devised an unusual tactic for conduct-ing warfare. The Persians expected to crush the Scythians in a decisive engagement, but the Scythians avoided such a battle. They retreated deep into their own territory, laying waste the region and wearing down the enemy by means of small raids. In pursuing the Scythians Darius soon came to appreciate the cunning of these "partisan" tactics. Reaching the Volga, Darius, acknowledging defeat, had to retreat from Scythia in shame.

As every student of military history knows, Napoleon and Hitler, each, in more modern times, encountered the same tactics from the Scythian descendants, and yielding similar results.

When Napoleon entered Russia in 1812, Field Marshall Kutuzov's similar strategy, including the sacrifice of Moscow itself, resulted in reducing Napoleon's Grande Armée from 453,000 to less than 10,000, and yielding the ignomious defeat now commemorated in Tchaikovsky's *Overture of 1812*.

In 1941, Hitler suffered a similar defeat from the same Scythian strategy: allowing a quick advance deep into the Russian interior only to have his *Wehrmacht* swallowed up in the harsh Russian winter.

The Scythian State

The creation of an enormous Scythian state began a new phase of their history. Herodotus describes Scythia as a square, 20 days journey (360 miles) on a side. It encompassed the lower reaches of the Dniester, Bug, Dnieper, and Don Rivers where they flow into the Black Sea and the Sea of Azov.[60]

It was the nature of the Scythians to always be waging small wars. They regularly carried out raids against the Sindi along the River Kuban, crossing the Cimmerian Bosphorus

(Kerch Strait) on the ice[61]. In 496 B.C. they raided beyond the Danube as far as Thracian Chersonesus on the Sea of Marmara.

The large Scythian state was organized as several large tribal alliances, each ruled by a king. During the war between the Scythians and the Persians, Herodotus names three kings, the chief of whom was Idanthyrsus. It appears that in the 4th century B.C. a single autocracy was set up under King Atheas. Coinage surviving portrays their king as a mounted archer, holding a bow and bearing his name, as a symbol of the unified state and a unique declaration of power.

King Atheas strived to extend the boundaries of his state. Scythian power reached beyond the Danube to the lands of the Thracian tribes. Scythia was prevented from reaching beyond Danube by Macedonia, which occupied the northeastern portion of the Balkan peninsula.

In 339 B.C., a great battle took place between the Scythians, led by the 90-year-old Atheas, and the Macedonians under the supreme command of Philip II (the father of the celebrated Alexander the Great), in which the Scythian forces were defeated and King Atheas was killed. Even after this, the struggle between Scythia and Macedonia continued.

In 331 B.C., Alexander's second-in-command, Zopyrion, attacked Olbia with a large force. The town withstood a siege and the 30,000 strong army of Zopyrion was defeated by the Scythians.

In 292 B.C. the Scythians, in alliance with the Thracian tribes of Goths, even routed the forces of Lysimachus, the ruler of Thrace.

However, in the 3rd century B.C. Scythian power declined significantly. There were several causes, the main one was apparently ecological. Evidently the natural and climatic conditions of life on the steppe were changing. According to some experts there was a "desertification" of the steppe.[62]

The population moved to more favorable areas, in particular southwards to the southern Dnieper. Greater Scythia disintegrated in the late 3rd century B.C., and the territory now only extended from the Lower Dnieper to the Crimea. The town called Neapolis became the capital of the new state. It was located on the River Salgir, and near it Simferopol later grew up. One other territory remained under Scythian control, near Dobruja beyond the Danube. The Scythians finally succumbed to attacks from the Goths.

Their history, stretching over almost a 1,000 years is stamped on what they left behind--not only in tangible remains but in many cultural influences.

The Scythians under the Persians

The Persians called the various Scythian tribes, *Saka*.[63] (Saka means "stag," a favorite animal of Scythian art and which may have had special religious significance as did the boar.)

Some of the Scythians were subjugated by the Persians and served in the Persian army against the Greeks. The Persians distinguished among three groups of *Saka* (Scythians):

1) *Saka tyaiy paradraya* ("beyond-the-sea Scythians"). The group in the west: to the north of the Black Sea in the Ukraine and to the west of the sea in Thrace.[64]

2) *Saka haumavarga* (named from Scythians who ate the hallucinogenic "haoma" plant; or, possibly, from a leader named *hu-marga*, "he who has good plains"). These Scythians have been located in Central Asia south of Lake Balkhash in the Ili Valley near the Pamir Mountains, and also between the Syr Dar'ya (Jaxartes) and Amu Dar'ya (Oxus) Rivers, which flow into the Aral Sea.[65]

3) *Saka tigrachauda* ("pointed-hat Scythians").[66] These were in the east, just to the west of the *Saka haumavarga,* in the area between the Caspian and the Aral Seas.[67]

From Herodotus we learn that Scythians formed an important part of the great army of Xerxes which invaded Greece in 480.[68]

The Scythians under the Greeks

The Scythians were opportunistic: they were ready to change sides as it suited them. We find them for and against the Urartians, for and against the Assyrians, for and against the Egyptians, etc.

Not only did some of the Scythians fight against the Greeks, other Scythians served under them. We have more than 400 representations of Scythian archers on ancient Greek vase paintings The earliest occur in the early 6th century; the bulk of them from 530 to 490 B.C.

The Scythians under the Romans

The Scythians were gradually overwhelmed by a kindred tribe, the Sarmatians. The process was complete by the 3rd century B.C. Herodotus called the latter the Sauromatae.[69] He located them to the east of the Scythians beyond the Don River (ancient Tanais).[70] Their original home was on either side of the Volga between the Don and the Ural.[71]

The Scythians were able to hang on to a restricted "kingdom" in the Crimean peninsula until the late 3rd century A.D., when they were overrun by the Goths.[72]

Scythians in the New Testament

The word *Scythian* occurs once in the New Testament. In Colossians 3:11, Paul stresses the fact that people from the most diverse backgrounds can be one in Christ:

> *Where there is neither Greek nor Jew, circumcision nor uncircumcision, Barbarian, Scythian, bond nor free: but Christ is all, and in all.*

(Almost all translations simply render the Greek Σκύθης, "Scythian," without any further comment.[73] Phillips and Way substitute "savage." The Amplified Version appends M. R. Vincent's comments in brackets, "who are the most savage of all." The Living Bible in its free paraphrase loses all reference to the original ethnic terms.)

Unfortunately modern commentaries scarcely do justice to the profound implications the term had for the original readers of the New Testament, devoting either a sentence[74] or at best a paragraph to the term.[75] One of the fullest treatments may be found in the classic commentary of J. B. Lightfoot, who includes many classical and patristic references to the Scythians.[76]

The usual association which the word *Scythian* suggested in antiquity was *savagery*. The writer of II Maccabees 4:47 (1st century B.C.) says of the injustice of Ptolemy VI (172-145 B.C.):

> *"He sentenced to death those unfortunate men, who would have been freed uncondemned if they had pleaded even before Scythians . . . "*

That is, even before those as cruel as Scythians. III Maccabees 7:5 (1st century B.C.) describes the Egyptian Jews' treatment of those of their number who had apostatized:

> *"And they, bringing them bound with harsh treatment as slaves, or rather traitors, without any enquiry or examination, attempted to put them to death, girding themselves with a cruelty fiercer than Scythian customs."*

In highlighting the agony of one of the seven sons who were martyred for their faith, IV Maccabees 10:7 (1st century A.D.) relates:

> *"And being in no way able to choke his spirit, they flayed off his skin with the tips of his fingers and stripped off his scalp as the Scythians do."*

Josephus[77] notes,

> *"But even Scythians, who delight in murdering people and are little better than wild beasts, nevertheless think it their duty to uphold their national customs."*

In a passage in which he denounces the gory gladiatorial games, Tertullian refers to the Scythians:

> *"As for bloody food and such tragic dishes, read--I think it is related by Herodotus [4.70], but I am not sure--how, among some tribes, blood was taken from the arms and tasted by both parties in forming a treaty . . . And they say that it was a custom among certain tribes of Scythians for every deceased member to be eaten by his relatives.* "[78]

These unsavory associations, then, provide the point of the reference to the Scythians in Colossians 3:11, a word which means nothing to readers today but which would have aroused a strong emotional response from Paul's audience. According to this passage, not only were all classes of society, civilized and uncivilized, one in Christ, but even those cruel, barbaric Scythians--*the epitome of savagery in the ancient world*--were eligible for redemption through the grace of our Lord Jesus Christ.

Even as you and I are. No matter how barbaric or cruel our own history is, His redemption is available for the asking.

Summary

The primary identity involved in Ezekiel 38 and 39 is the land of Magog which all ancient authorities clearly identify as the Scythians, which, in turn, are the ancestors of the present day Russians.

This critical identification is the key to understanding this remarkable passage and to recognizing its imminent fulfillment on today's prophetic horizon.

Since most of our readers may not be as familiar with the history of the region as we are that of Western Europe, it will be useful to survey it in the next couple of chapters.

Endnotes:

1. It is interesting to notice how frequently a woman is linked with a serpent: Genesis 3; the legends surrounding the birth of Alexander the Great, etc.

2. See R. G. Kent, *Old Persian,* 2nd ed., American Oriental Society, New Haven CT, 1953, p. 6; J. Potratz, *Die Skythen in Sudrussland,* Raggi, Basel, 1963, p. 17.

3. See "Scythian", Большая Советская Энциклопедия, *Great Soviet Encylopedia,* 3rd ed., 1979, vol 23, pp 259-260. Also, Herodotus 4.117, 4.108, 4.106.

4. Herodotus 4.17-18.

5. Rybakov, Геродотова Скифия, p. 117.

6. Herodotus 4.19

7. Ibid., 4.20.

8. Ibid., 4.17.

9. Ibid., 4.17.

10. Ibid., 4.116-117.

11. Ibid., 4.20, 107.

12. Ibid., 4.104.

13. Ibid., 4.108-109.

14. Ibid., 4.105.

15. Ibid., 4.121, 108-109.

16. Ibid., 4.18, 106.

17. Ibid., 4.22.

18. Ibid., 4.22. See also Rybakov, pp. 17, 107, 147, 161, 165, 191.; T. Sulimirski, "The Scythian Age in the U.S.S.R.," *Bulletin of the Institute of Archaeology,* London, 10, 1971, pp. 104-105.

19. M. Van Loon, review of J. Potratz, Die Skythen in Sudrussland, in *Journal of Near Eastern Studies,* 29, 1970, p. 71.

20. Rybakov, Геродотова Скифия, pp. 104-168; T. Sulimirski, "The Scythian Age int the U.S.S.R.,"*Bulletin of the Institute of Archaeology,* London, 10, 1971, pp. 114-131; V. S. Olkhovski, "The Scythian Catacombs in the Steppes of the Black Sea",

Советская Археология, (Sovetskaia Arkheologiia), no. 4, 1977, pp. 108-128; idem, ""The Ancient Tombs of the Scyths According to Herodotus and the Archaeological Data", Советская Археология, (Sovietskaia Arkheologiia), No. 4, 1978, pp. 83-97. A valuable summary is A. M. Leskov, "Die skythischen Kurgane," *Antike Welt* 5, Sondernummer; 1974.

21.   M. I. Artamonov, *The Splendor of Scythian Art: Treasures from the Scythian Tombs,* Praeger, NY, 1969; idem. *Treasures from the Scythian Tombs in the Hermitage Museum,* Thames and Hudson, London, 1969.

22.   M. Griaznov and E. Golomstock, "The Pazirik Burials of the Altai," *American Journal of Archaeology,* 37, 1933, pp. 30-45.

23.   S. I. Rudenko, *Frozen Tombs of Siberia: The Pazyryk Burials of Iron-Age Horsemen,* University of California, Berkeley, 1970. Also, T. Sulimirski, "The Late Bronze Age and Earliest Iron Age in Siberia," *Bulletin of the Institute of Archaeology,* 12, London, 1975, pp. 152-153.

24.   "Experts struggle to preserve 2,500-year-old Horseman," *Orange County Register,* Sept 1, 1995.

25.   "Nemirov Gorodische",Большая Советская Энциклопедия, 3rd ed., 1978, vol 17, p. 427.

26.   A. M. Leskov, "Die skythischen Kurgane," *Antike Welt,* 5, Sondernummer; 1974.

27.   R. Ghirshman, *The Art of Ancient Iran,* Golden Press, NY, 1964, p. 98; suggests that the name *Sakkez* preserves the Persian name of the Scythian, *Saka.*

28.   R. Ghirshman, "A propos du tresor de Ziwiye," *Journal of Near Eastern Studies,* 32, 1973, pp. 445-452.

29.   Probably the *Protothyes* of Herodotus 1.103.

30.   A. T. Olmstead, *History of Assyria,* 2nd ed., University of Chicago, Chicago, 1951, p. 361.

31.   R. Ghrishman, *Tombe Princiere de Ziwiye et le debut de l'art animalier scythe,* La Societe Iranienne pour la Conversation due Patrimoine National, Paris, 1979, pp. 9-10; T. Sulimirski, "The Background of the Ziwiye Find and Its Significance in the Development of Scythian Art,", *Bulletin of the Institute of Archaelology,* London, 15, 1978, pp. 7-13.

32.   Herodotus 1.103.

33.   Ibid., 4.1.

34.   D. I. Page, *History and the Homeric Iliad,* Univesity of California, Berkely, 1959, p. 104.

35. D. Georgacas, "The Name Asia for the Continent," Names 17, 1969, p. 90; *The Names for the Asia Minor Peninsula,* Carl Winter, Heidelberg, 1971.

36. T. Rice, *Scythians,* p. 42; Rybakov, *Gerodotova Skifiia,* pp. 239-240; M. I. Artamonov, *Treasures from Scythian Tombs in the Hermitage Museum,* Thames and Hudson, London, 1969, p. 16; K. S. Rubinson, "Herodotus and the Scythians," *Expedition,* 17, Summer, 1975, p. 20; T. Sulimirski, "Scythian Antiquities,", p. 294, citing works of C. F. Lehmann-Haupt, V. Struve, G. C. Cameron, and A. Baschmakoff in support of Herodotus. Also, J. Przyluski, "Noveaux aspects de l'histoire des Scythes," *Revue de l'Universite de Bruxelles,* 42, 1936-1937, pp. 210ff.

37. Herodotus, 4.46.

38. M. Rostovtzeff, "The Parthian Shot" *American Journal of Archaelology,* 47, 1943, pp. 174-187.

39. A.D.H. Bivar, "Calvary Equipment and Tactics on the Euphrates Frontier," *Dumbarton Oaks Papers* 26, 1972, p. 274. Denis Sinor, "The Inner Asian Warriors," *Journal of the American Oriental Society,* 101, 1981, pp. 137-138.

40. E. D. Phillips, "New Light on the Ancient History of the Eurasian Steppe," *American Journal of Archaeology,* 61, 1957, p. 274.

41. Vos, *Scythian Archers,* pp. 40-47.

42. Y. Yadin, *The Art of Warfare in Biblical Lands,* Weidenfeld and Nicolson, London, 1963, pp. 196-197. cf I Kings 22:34-35.

43. T. Sulimirski, *Prehistoric Russia,* Humanities Press, New York, 1970; Y. Yadin, *The Art of Warfare in Biblical Lands,* Weidenfeld and Nicolson, London, 1963, pp. 384-385.

44. Xenophon *Anabasis* 3.3.10; M. Rostovtzeff, "The Parthian Shot," American Journal of Archaeology, 47, 1943, pp. 180-181. This mode of shooting is depicted on a number of Greek black-figure vases.

45. T. Sulimirski, "Les archers a cheval, cavalerie legere des ancients," *Revue International d'Histoire Militaire* 3, 1952, p. 453; D. Sinor, "The Inner Asian Warriors," *Journal of the American Oriental Society,* 101, 1981, p. 135.

46. *Laws* 795A.

47. Hermotimos 33.

48. J. D. Lathan, "The Archers of the Middle East: The Turco-Iranian Background," *Iran* 8, 1970, p. 97 "...can shoot at beasts, birds, hoops, men, sitting quarry, dummies, and birds on the wing, and do so at full gallop to fore or to rear, to left or to right, upwards or downwards, loosing ten arrows before their enemies can nock one." Distances of up to 500 meters (1640 feet) were recorded at Olbia.

49. Herodotus 4.118-142. B. A. Rybakov, Геродотова Скифия, Nauka, Moscow, 1979, pp. 169-184.

50. J. F. C. Fuller, *The Generalship of Alexander the Great,* Rutgers University, New Brunswick NJ, 1960, pp. 239-242.

51. H. L. Lorimer, *Homer and the Monuments,* Macmillan, London, 1950, pp. 276-277.

52. Theoctitus 13.56. Sinor, "Inner Asian Warriors," p. 140, n.59.

53. M. F. Vos, *Scythian Archers,* J. B. Wolters, Goningen, 1963, p. 59, n.2; A. M. Snodgrass, *Arms and Armour of the Greeks,* Thames and Hudson, London, 1967, p. 83.

54. Vos, *Scythian Archers,* p. 49.

55. M. P. Gryaznov, *The Ancient Civilization of Souther Siberia,* Crowles, New York, 1969, p. 157; Grakow, *Die Skythen,* p. 80; Snodgrass, *Arms and Armor of the Greeks,* p.83; Vos, *Scythian Archers,* p. 49.

56. Grakow, *Die Skythen,* p. 81; Snodgrass, *Arms,* p. 83.

57. Leskov, "Die skythischen Kurgane," pp. 57-58; Grakov, *Die Skythen,* pp. 80-81; Vickers, *Scythian Treasures,* p. 34.

58. Herodotus, 1.106.

59. Ibid., 4.1.

60. B.A. Rybakov, Геродотова Скифия, (Herodotus's Scythia), Nauka, Moscow, 1979, p. 19.

61. Herodotus, 4, 28.

62. Some believe that orbital perturbations may have altered the Earth's ecological balance in ages past. See *Signs in the Heavens,* Koinonia House, for a discussion.

63. B. Brentjes, "Die Skythen und ihre Kunst--der Tierstil," *Das Altertum* 27.3, 1981; p. 15.

64. Kent, *Old Persian,* pp. 137, 195; W. Culican, *The Medes and Persians,* Praeger, New York, 1965, p. 73; S. Parlato, "La cosidetta campagna scitica di Dario," *Annali Istituto Orientale di Napoli,* 41, 1981, p. 246; R. Schmitt, "Die achaimenidische Satrapie Tayaiy Drayahya," *Historia* 21, 1972, pp. 522-527.

65. Culican, *Medes,* p. 73; Herzfeld, *Persian Empire,* pp. 327-329; Dandamarev, "Dannye Babilonskikh Documentov," p. 32.

66. Kent, *Old Persian,* p. 186.

67. Culican, *Medes,* p. 73; Parlato, "La Considetta campagna," p. 229; Harmatta, "Darius Expedition," pp. 16-17.

68. Herodotus 7.64.

69. Ibid., 4.117.

70. B. A. Rybakov, **Геродотова Скифия**, Nauka, Moscow, 1979, pp. 107-191.

71. E. D. Phillips, *The Royal Hordes: Nomad Peoples of the Steppes,* McGraw-Hill, New York, 1965, p. 92; W. M. McGovern, *The Early Empires of Central Asia,* University of North Carolina, Chapel Hill, 1939, ch. 2; T. Sulimirski, *The Sarmatians,* Thames and Hudson, London, 1970.

72. K. F. Smirnov, "Scythians," **Советская Археология**, 3rd ed., 1979, vol 23, p. 260.

73. *Berkeley, Goodspeed, Jerusalem Bible, New American Bible, New American Standard Bible, New English Bible, Revised Standard Version.*

74. C. Vaughn, "Colossians," in *The Expositor's Bible Commentary,* ed. F. E. Gaebelein, Zondervan, Grand Rapids MI, 1978, vol 11, p. 213.

75. F.F. Bruce, *Commentary on...Colossians,* Eerdmans, Grand Rapids, 1957, p. 276.

76. J. B. Lightfoot, *Commentary on Saint Paul's Epistles to the Colossians and Philemon,* Zondervan, 1957 (reprint of 1879 edition), pp. 218-219.

77. Josephus, *Contra Apionem* 2.269.

78. Apology 9.9. Origen (*Contra Celsum* 1.1) describes the laws of the Scythians as "unholy", "impious," and "despotic."

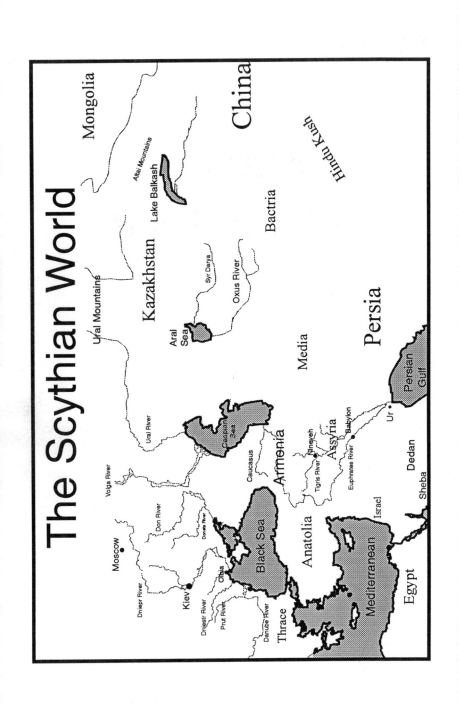

The Scythian World

Chapter 5:

Magog
of the East

And the sixth angel poured out his vial upon the great river Euphrates; and the water thereof was dried up, that the way of the kings of the east might be prepared.

Revelation 16:12

A review of the northern Black Sea, and the southern steppes in general, will be helpful in understanding the flow of history for the unfamiliar reader. These stormy events from a colorful but violent past, from the invasion by the Huns into the European steppes, the fall of the Western Roman Empire, and the appearance in Asia and Europe of the Turkish, Avar and Khazar Khanates, and the invasion by the armies of Genghis Khan and Batu will be summarized.

(The spread of ancient Slavs into Central Europe and the Balkans; their interminable struggle with Byzantium; and the foundation and growth of the first ancient Russian state, Kievan Rus, will be reviewed in chapter 6.)

The Hsiung-Nu

A powerful grouping of nomadic tribes which occupied lands now in northern China in the second half of the first millennium B.C. were known by the Chinese[1] as the Hsiung-Nu. To protect themselves from these aggressive raiders, the Chinese began to build the Great Wall along their northern frontiers in the late 4th century B.C. The Moslem writers in the 8th century refer to the Great Wall of China as *Sud Yagog et*

Magog, "the rampart of Gog and Magog."[2]   The Moslems refer to Gog and Magog as *Vadjudj wa madjudj* in the Koran.[3]

By degrees the Chinese drove the steppe tribes northwards beyond the Gobi Desert and into the steppes of modern Mongolia. In this area by the 3rd century B.C. the powerful Hsiung-Nu Empire had been created. Included in it were tribes in southern Siberia, Zabaykal, Mongolia, and Manchuria.

By the end of the 1st century A.D., following uninterrupted wars with China and also internal dissension, the empire of the Hsiung-Nu split into two parts, the southern and the northern.   The former came under the rule of the Chinese emperors, while the northern Hsiung-Nu left their territory in A.D. 93 and began the "Great Raid" into the West. They ruled Central Asia for more than 200 years. During this time they clashed with local Iranian-speaking tribes, the Sakas, Massagetae, and Issidones, with ancient Turkish and Ugrian tribes, and other peoples. Some of them were exterminated or driven out, and others were assimilated.

The main language of this conglomeration of tribes was a Turkish tongue.   The Turkic peoples are historically and linguistically linked with T'uchüeh, the name given by the Chinese to the nomad peoples who founded their empire stretching from Mongolia and the northern frontier of China to the Black Sea. (The name originated from that of one of the khans of the Golden Horde who embraced Islam. They were all Muslim. This will be reviewed shortly.)

The Huns

In A.D. 375 the enormous mass of various Asian tribes,

centered on the military power of the Hsiung-Nu, once more took up their drive westwards. In Europe they became known as the Huns.

Evidences from archaeology and written sources show that from the second half of the 4th century to the first half of the 5th, over the whole southern Ukrainian steppe a new culture arose among the nomads in the great migrations period. Crossing the Volga and Don, the Huns invaded the steppes of the northern Black Sea area.

At this time the area was ruled over by two tribal alliances: the German Goths and the Iranian-speaking Sarmatians. After a ferocious battle the Huns emerged victorious. While assimilating some of the Goths and Sarmatians and building up their strength for a new campaign, the Huns remained in the East European steppes until 420. They then crossed the Danube and advanced to the borders of Western Europe, plundering and laying waste everything en route. They laid siege to Constantinople in 434, but yielded when they were given a large ransom. Eventually they made the Central Danube steppes (Pannonia) their base.

In 445 Attila became the leader of the Huns. His rule of the new nomad empire marked a period of great activity in Europe. It waged devastating wars with neighboring countries, inspiring terror in their peoples. Provinces of the Western and Eastern Roman empires[4] were laid waste.[5]   The Huns raided right up to the banks of the Rhine, to Strasbourg and Orleans, and more than once threatened Constantinople. For its dependable rear the Hunnish Empire relied on the northern Black Sea area--nomadic tribes that had joined the Hun army and remained behind when the main force had left constituted an inexhaustible military reserve.

In 450 the Huns carried out a large incursion into Gaul. At Maurica in 451 (near Paris) there took place one of the greatest battles of antiquity. The Huns were opposed by an alliance of Romans, Gauls, and German tribes settled in Gaul within the Western Roman Empire. The battle was indecisive. However, Attila ordered a retreat and they returned to Pannonia. In 454 the Hunnish Empire dissolved when Attila died.

The Hun invasion radically changed the southern part of Eastern Europe. As well as sparking off the "Great Migrations" of many European peoples, the steppe zone was occupied by Turkish-speaking tribes who killed off, drove out, or assimilated the former Iranian-speaking population of Scythian and Sarmatians.

The old centers of culture--the Greek colonies of the northern Black Sea area, which had now become Byzantine provinces--were almost entirely destroyed by the barbarians of the first years of the Hun expansion. The ancient Slav tribes were also subjected to territorial ravages and were forced to move away into the forests to the north and northeast.

The Avars

After the demise of the Hunnish Empire many nomadic tribes in the northern Black Sea area, no longer finding themselves under a central authority, quarreled with each other and were unable to combine in a powerful tribal alliance to create a new empire on the steppes.

In the middle of the 6th century, Turkish-speaking tribes

of nomads, called in Europe the Avars, crossed the Volga and Don from Central Asia and invaded the southern Ukrainian steppes. Some of the local tribes joined the Avar alliance as a result of which the Avars became much more numerous and powerful. During their occupation of the Black Sea area they waged constant war with local nomadic and ancient Slav tribes who had once more occupied their lands after the departure of the Huns into Western Europe. Some of these Slav tribes were forcibly incorporated into the Avar alliance.

In 565 the united Avar forces crossed the Danube and invaded Byzantine territory. In 568 they became overlords of the Central Danube steppes. By the late 6th century a nomad military state made up of various tribes--the Avar Khanate--had arisen, at the core of which were the Avars.

At its head was the Khan Bayan. Contemporaries described him as a ruthless and skillful commander. The political history of the Avars in the Danube period recalls that of the Huns. It is a history of uninterrupted raids and military conflicts with the Franks and with Byzantium, and relentless plundering of the conquered peoples: the southern Slavs, Gepids and others. However, in the mid-7th century the Avar Khanate crumbled under the impact of Frankish assaults and internecine dissension, and as a military and political force it ceased to exist.

The development and introduction of new weapons technology is always one of the factors which gave rapid successes, to the Avars in this case, when they first burst onto the historical scene.

Avar weaponry is distinguished by a number of novel

characteristics. As before, the main weapon of the nomads was the bow and arrow, although the Avar bows were considerably larger and longer range. The spears, too, were longer and heavier. Replacing the straight, double-edged swords of the Sarmatians and Huns, there was introduced, in the 6th and 7th centuries the scimitar, a longer, slightly curved single-bladed sabre, intended for glancing blows.

All of these military innovations were possible thanks to the stirrup, which gave the rider more stability and, accordingly, a greater chance of success in hand-to-hand combat on horseback.

The Khazars

In the 7th and 8th centuries the northern Black Sea area steppes became part of one of the most powerful European states of the time: the Khazar Khanate. Its capital was Itil on the Lower Volga. The Khanate was of the semi-nomadic type and comprised many tribes practicing animal breeding, trade and manufacture. The dominant tribe was the Turkish-speaking Khazars. Military raids, the seizure of new lands, and political alliances with Byzantium played an important part in establishing the political and economic strength of the khanate.

The most dramatic occurrence of the seventh century was the rise of Muhammad and Islam in Arabia. In 680 an extended war began with the Arabs over the supremacy in Transcaucasia.

A powerful onslaught on Transcaucasia was called for, not only in the Khazars' own interests, but also at the instigation of Byzantium, which was faced by a mortal threat from the Muslims in Asia Minor. In the end, the Khazars were victorious in this ferocious war. If it had not turned out thus, the subsequent history of Eastern Europe might have been very different. The spread of Islam, and with it eastern civilization, was held up for several centuries at Europe's threshold in the Caucasus. The Khazars blocked the Islam's way, just as the Franks under Charles Martel were to do at Poitiers.

It is interesting that the agenda of Islam again clouds the horizon of world history. This time it has the resources-- nuclear weapons--to attempt to disconnect the Middle East from its Judeo-Christian roots. Unless God Himself intervenes, as Ezekiel describes. The origin, agenda, and rise of Islam will be reviewed in chapter 9.

After consolidating their position in the Caucasus, by the mid-8th century the Khazar state had extended its power over the whole of the southern part of East Europe from the southern Urals to the Danube, over the Finno-Ugrian and Turkish peoples of the Volga, and also over territories to the north of the steppes which belonged to the ancient Slav tribes. This was a period in which the nomad state flourished both politically, economically, and culturally.

In the late 8th century, heathenism of the Khazar Khanate was exchanged for a new state religion: Judaism. It was accepted mainly by the upper strata in society: the khan and his circle. The chieftains of the individual tribes did not accept it, but remained heathen. As a result of religious dissension, a civil war broke out that lasted for about a century. This lead to serious weakening of the Khanate, which was exploited by Asian nomads: the Magyars and Pechenegs.

At the end of the 9th century they invaded Khazar territory

and gradually whittled away the Khazars' power. The last blow against the khanage was wielded by Kievan Rus in the second half of the 10th century, and it ceased to exist following military campaigns by the Kievan princes in 965 and 969. (The rise of the Kievan Rus state will be reviewed in chapter 6.)

Throughout the whole history of the Khazars, trade was an important part of their lives, exports and imports being of equal importance. Customs duties collected from trade caravans crossing their territory and tribute from subject peoples also strengthened the state's economy. The Byzantine Empire exerted a huge influence on all aspects of Khazar society.

The Pechenegs and Polovtsky

After the final collapse of the Khazar Khanate, the southern Ukrainian steppes came under the rule of the Pechenegs (10th and first half of the 11th centuries) and then of the Polovtsky (mid 11th and first half of the 13th centuries). The Pecheneg armies first appeared in the northern Black Sea area steppes in the late 9th century. By the beginning of the 10th century they had completely taken over the territory between the Don and the Danube. Their original homeland was the steppes of Central Asia north of the Aral Sea.

The whole period of Pecheneg supremacy was marked by their plundering raids on the Byzantine provinces in the Crimea (Bosphorus and Khersonesus), Bulgaria, Hungary, Kievan Rus, and the land of the people living along the Don and Volga and in the northern Caucasus. In 1036 the united Pecheneg armies were routed by Rus forces near Kiev. After this defeat the main mass of nomads went west beyond the Danube. What remained of the Pechenegs partly went into the service of the Kievan princes, while others were annihilated by the new nomadic invaders: the Polovtsky.

The Polovtsky stemmed from the steppes of northern Kazakhstan and southern Siberia. Having dealt with the rump of the Pechenegs, they acquired the dominant role in the East European steppes from the Volga to the Danube. For two centuries the Polovtsian armies carried out repeated raids into neighboring territories. They frequently crossed the Danube and invaded Central Europe, ravaging the southern lands of Kievan Rus.

The ancient Rus state succeeded in repulsing the Polovtsian incursions. The Kievan princes directed the struggle against the Polovsty which continued from the mid-11th to the mid-13th century, when the Polovtsian state was destroyed by the Mongols. Some of the Polovtsky joined the Mongol's tribal alliance.

The Mongols and the Golden Horde

In the early 13th century, a very powerful Mongol nomad state was founded in Central Asia under Genghis Khan. One of the chief constituent tribes was the Mongols, also known as the Tatars. Beginning in 1206, the Mongol armies seized northern China, Manchuria, and territories in southeastern Siberia, Central and southwestern Asia, and East Europe.

By 1242, nomad armies, under the command of Khan Batu (grandson of Genghis Khan), after devastating and subjugating many Asian and European states, reached the borders of North Italy and Germany. Such a threat from steppe nomads had not faced Europe since the invasion of the Huns.

However, in late 1242, at the most critical moment for Western Europe, Khan Batu turned his armies about and headed east to the Volga steppes.[6]

As a result of aggressive campaigns, three western branches of the empire founded by Genghis Khan emerged. For a while, they were dependent upon the great Khan of the Mongols in their capital Karkorum in Mongolia, but later they became independent states. The largest of the three was the domain of Jochi, the eldest son of Genghis Khan. It included West Siberia, the Priural and Volga region, the northern Caucasus, the Crimea, northern Khoresm, the lands of the Polovtsky and other tribes and peoples living on the vast steppes from the Irtysh to the Danube. Jochi's domain, subsequently named the Golden Horde, was founded by Khan Batu in 1243. Its capital was the town of Sarai on the Lower Volga.

The ancient Slav state did not join the Golden Horde, although it was largely dependent upon it, and paid an annual tribute to the Mongol khans.

The Golden Horde was one of the most powerful states of Eurasia in the 13th and first half of the 14th centuries. It lasted more than 200 years, eventually disintegrating into separate states: the Kazan, Astrakhan, Siberian and Crimean Khanates, as a result of internecine conflict and the growing power of the princes in Moscow (The *Muscoi*, et al.).

The cultural characteristics of the enormous multiethnic alliance were determined by the political, economic, and social peculiarities of life in the state. This was expressed in the interaction of the steppe nomads' culture with the syncretic culture of the towns, which were populated not only by Mongols, but also by Polovtsky, Bulgars, Russians, Finno-Ugrian people from the Volga region and the Urals, immigrants from Western Europe and Central Asia, Iran, the Crimea, the Caucasus, China, India, et al. They were responsible for creating the urban culture, at the core of which appeared the traditions and artistic characteristics of the settled and highly developed civilizations of the native peoples.

The emergence of modern Russia is continued in the next chapter.

Endnotes:

1.   In Genesis 10:17; 1 Chronicles 1:15; and Isaiah 49:12 we have allusions to the
      Sinites and Sinim, which some scholars believe may refer to the Chinese ("sino-")
      peoples.

2.   Kesses HaSofer, *Bereishis - Genesis,* A New Translation with a Commentary
      Anthologised from Talmudic, Midrashic and Rabbinic Sources, Mesorah Publica-
      tions, Lt.

3.   Koran, 21:96.

4.   The two "legs" of the vision of Daniel 2?

5.   This began the fragmentation of the empire which would ultimately regather as the
      European Suprastate. See *Iron Mixed With Clay*, Koinonia House.

6.   The Bible indicates that the boundaries of nations are determined by God. Daniel
      4:17; Deuteronomy 32:8; Job 14:5; Acts 17:26.

Chapter 6:

The Rus Emerge

Son of man, set thy face toward Gog, of the land of Magog, the prince of Rosh (Rus), Meshech, and Tubal, and prophesy against him...

Ezekiel 38:2 (ASV)

The background that has endowed these vibrant people with the beauty of Pushkin, Dostoyevsky, and Tchaikovsky, has also given them the cruelty of Ivan IV,[1] the intensity of Lenin, the brutality of Stalin, and the deceit of Gorbachev.

The Ancient East Slavs

In European history the second half of the first millennium was a period of great disruptions. The migrations of many peoples and their struggle with the Roman Empire on its western borders came to an end, while in the east, on the borders of the Byzantine Empire, they continued into the 6th and 7th centuries. This period was very important for the history of the Slavs, and their significance on the European political stage rapidly increased.

There is plentiful evidence to suggest that their original homeland was between the Middle Dnieper and basin of the Vistula, and possibly also that of the Oder. Their economy was based on agriculture, and from it sprang animal breeding. Hunting, fishing and bee keeping also played an important role, since the natural conditions were favorable to them.

Together with other tribes they carried on a prolonged struggle with the Byzantine Empire during the 6th and 7th centuries. This period has become known as the Balkan Wars. Numerous raids by the Slavs over the imperial borders were accompanied by the migration of a considerable proportion of the Slav people to the Balkan Peninsula, which they almost took over entirely. These tribes moved from their homeland not only southwestwards in the direction of the Danube and Balkans, but also west, reaching the Elbe, and north to the Gulf of Finland, and east to the Upper Volga. This widespread migration led to the separation of the East, West, and South Slavs, which was essentially completed in the second half of the first millennium.

The East Slavs settled in territory bordering the Carpathians in the west, the Gulf of Finland in the North, the Upper Volga in the east, and the northern Black Sea steppes in the south, the latter occupied by nomads. During the Slav migrations, a large alliance of tribes emerged in East Europe which subsequently took the form of a military and political state. The Middle Dnieper region played an important role in the history of the East Slavs. It was occupied by Poles and was to become the nucleus of the future ancient Russian state, the Kievan Rus.

The Poles were the most powerful element in the tribal alliance, which neighboring tribes also joined. Located on the edge of the forest-steppe, this alliance played a very important role in the life of all the Slav tribes along the Dnieper. For instance, in a fierce struggle, it withstood the onslaught of the steppe nomads--the Avars, Bulgars, Khazars, and others--and this helped to create the conditions for an intensive development of the economy and culture.

As a result of the development of manufacture and trade among the Eastern Slavs, in particular the Middle Dnieper region in the 6th and 7th centuries, towns arose which functioned as manufacturing, trading and tribal centers. One of these settlements became the capital of the Polish tribal alliance and the center of Rus. Thus, were laid the foundations of Kiev.

The Prince of Rosh

One of the incidental translation problems in Ezekiel 38 deals with *Rosh:* in some instances, it is transliterated as a proper name;[2] in others, it is translated as the title, "Chief."[3]

There are some experts who hold the view that it is from the same root as *Rus,* (also spelled Ros), which was the name for the indigenous Slavs of the southern steppes,[4] and the root from which *Russia* eventually got its name.

The Rurik Dynasty

Traditions in the West have ascribed the Rus as descendants of the Varangians, Scandinavian Vikings who ruled Novgorod in the latter part of the 9th century. Princes of Kievan Rus and, later, Muscovy, according to tradition, were descendants of the Varangian Prince Rurik who ruled that city in 862 A.D.

However, more recent Russian scholarship considers the Rus to be a southeastern Slavic tribe that founded a tribal league. The Rus were simply a southern Slavic tribe living on the Ros River. The Kievan state, they affirm, was the creation of the Slavs and was attacked and held only briefly by the Varangians.[5]

The Cyrillic Alphabet

The Greek alphabet, created in 1st millennium B.C., is the basis of all alphabets in Europe today, directly or indirectly.

The Old Slavonic Language[6] was based on Macedonian (south Slavic) dialects from around Thessalonica. The Cyrillic alphabet, based on the Greek uncial script of the 9th century, was invented by two Greek brothers, St. Cyril and St. Methodius, natives of Thessalonica, for preaching to the Moravian Slavs and for translating the Bible into Slavic. It originally consisted of 43 letters, based on Greek letters and 2 Hebrew letters (צ, *tsade* and ש, *shin*, for ch, sh, and shch). (Modern Cyrillic alphabets, Russian, Ukrainian, Bulgarian, and Serbian, have been modified, dropping some superfluous letters. Russian now has 32 letters; Bulgarian 30, Serbian 30, and Ukrainian 33.)

This first Slavic literary language was written in two alphabets (known as Glagolitic and Cyrillic) where it remained the religious and literary language of Orthodox Slavs throughout the Middle Ages, and is currently used in Russia, Bulgaria, and Serbia. Thus, two alphabets are used for writing Slavic languages, Cyrillic and Latin. Cyrillic is used by those Slavic peoples who accepted their religion from Byzantium; Roman Christianity brought the use of Latin to the Poles, Lusatians, Czechs, Slovaks, Slovenes, and Croats.

(In Yugoslavia, a single language is written differently by the Catholic Croats and the Greek Orthodox Serbs. The tensions and violence visible today have deep roots.)

Kievan Rus

As already mentioned, from the 7th to the first half of the 9th centuries large tribal alliances were set up in the eastern Slav lands. They reflect the process of forming a state among the East Slavs. At this time new circumstances arose, including the advanced development of the economy, in particular, agriculture and manufacturing, which accelerated the collapse of earlier tribal relations.

Various trading links with the Arabian East and Byzantium, the necessity of defending their land from raids by steppe nomads, and the general improvement of the economy brought about favorable conditions of the last quarter of the 9th century for the setting up of a common eastern Slav state. The unification of the northern (based on Novgorod) and southern (Kievan) lands, which occurred under Prince Oleg (882-911) completed the formation of the first ancient Russian state, Kievan Rus. Its capital was Kiev, which had been founded in the late 5th or early 6th century.

Kievan Rus, which during the 10th century united all the eastern Slav tribes, became one of the most powerful European states of the time. The culmination of its historical development was reached during the reign of Prince Vladimir Sviatoslavich (978-1015). He was one of the most talented rulers of his period. He devoted all his energies to the unification and consolidation of the state. In 988 Prince Vladimir accepted Christianity which in time became the state religion. In ousting pagan beliefs, Christianity assisted in the extension and strengthening of political, economic and cultural relations with other countries in Europe and the East. It also assisted in the stabilization of relations between its own lands, and the new religion furthered the extensive penetration into Rus of the influence of the advanced Byzantine culture, which in turn encouraged the development of the literature, architecture and art already exiting in the country.

After Vladimir's death, the Kievan throne was occupied by his son Yaroslav, known amongst the people as "The Wise." This great prince (1019-1054) continued his father's policies. His rule was marked by a further improvement in the fortunes of Rus and its capital. At the same time the state was expanding toward the Baltic and the Carpathians. Yaroslav had Kiev surrounded by strong defenses. Monumental buildings were erected within the city: churches, cathedrals and palaces, and it became a great political, economic and cultural center in East Europe. Foreign merchants and travelers compared Kiev in its beauty and opulence to the capital of Byzantium, Constantinople.

Kievan Rus maintained friendly relations with many other countries--Byzantium, Germany, France, Hungary, Poland, Scandinavia, the Khazar Khanate, the Volga Bulgars, etc. During the rule of Yaroslav the Wise, the threat arose of an invasion by the Pechenegs from the steppe.   In 1036 they were finally beaten in a battle near Kiev.

At the end of the 11th century, Yaroslav's grandson, Prince Vladimir Monomakh, entered the political arena. During his reign he attempted to preserve the political unity of all the lands of ancient Rus. He also organized, with other princes, successful raids against the steppe armies of the Polovtsy, whose attacks were increasing. By that time the prestige of Kievan Rus on the international scene had grown enormously. Relations with neighboring states were particularly strengthened. The original and distinctive culture of the Kievan Rus had an outstanding influence on the development of world culture.

Rus lay at the crossroads of trade routes between Scandinavia and Byzantium. The cultural achievements of the Kievan Rus deeply influenced the subsequent achievements of Ukrainian, Russian, and Belorussian peoples.

The development of ancient Rus was interrupted by the Mongol invasion, reviewed in the previous chapter. After the Mongol invasion (1240) the Russian princes were obliged to seek a patent from the Mongol khan in order to rule as the grand prince. Rivalry developed between the princely houses and eventually the princes of Moscow became dominant, forming the Grand Principality of Moscow (Muscovy), which they ruled until their male line died out in 1598.

The House of Romanov

In 1472, Ivan III ("The Great") married the daughter of the last of the Byzantine emperors and also adopted the Byzantine double eagle as the symbol of Czarist Russia.

The golden two-headed eagle had been in use in Egypt in the 7th century B.C. and later became the emblem of the Byzantine Empire. Facing east and west, this appeared to be an appropriate symbol for the empire straddling the antitheses of the East and the West.

(See page 244 for a depiction of this classic symbol.)

When Fyodor I (the last ruler of the Rurik dynasty) died in 1598, Russia endured 15 chaotic years known as the Time of Troubles (1598-1613) which ended when a *zemsky sobor* ("assembly of the land") elected Michael Romanov as the new Czar.   The two-headed eagle was used by the Romanov Dynasty until Czar Nicholas II was executed by the Bolsheviks in July 1918.

(The surprising resurrection of this ancient symbol in 1994 will be discussed in Chapter 15.)

The Bolshevik Revolution

Capitalizing on the repressive reign of the Czars,[7] and the turmoil of the war years, in October of 1917, the Bolsheviks ("One of the Majority") seized power and inaugurated the Soviet regime.

The 70 years of Communist rule--with its enforced athiesm--is familiar enough to most of our readers so we will forego summarizing it here.

The Soviet Enigma

However, the growing strength of the USSR and the apparent threat of world Communism, continued to be a major puzzle to perceptive Biblical commentators since the classic Biblical scenarios--as summarized in Daniel chapters 2 and 7--profiled only four great world empires from the Babylon of Daniel's time to the time when God would intervene in history and establish His own kingdom upon the earth. Only four empires were in view: Babylon, Persia, Greece and Rome (in two phases).

The fourth empire, Rome, was never conquered. It disintegrated into pieces about 476 A.D. Each of the "pieces" has made a bid for world dominion, but none really made it. Charlemagne, Napoleon, Bismark, Hitler, et al., all had "their day in the sun," but never quite recovered the glory that was Rome. Daniel's passages predict that, at the "end time," the former elements would recombine to once again form a dominant European Suprastate which will figure prominently in the Biblical scenario. This, too, has been coming, like a glacier, over the past 40 years.[8]

The apparent emergence of the Soviet Empire was an enigma from a Biblical viewpoint. What was going to stop them?

In August 1991, we got our answer.

The Fall of the Soviet Union

In remarkable compliance to the strategy outlined by the classic Russian strategists--from Manuilski to Gorbachev--the apparent collapse of the Soviet Union emerged on the world scene.

The three-day *coup* that appeared to herald the demise of the evil empire is now regarded by some observers as simply a charade for Western consumption. There are those who believe that it was part of the deceptive "theatre" that makes up Russian politics.

There have been six periods of "*glasnost/perestroika*'s" since the 1920's. The first was from 1921 - 1929 under Lenin. The next was 1936-1937 under Stalin. The next was 1941-

1945 under Stalin.   The fourth was 1956 - 1959 under Kruschev.   The fifth was 1970 - 1975 under Beshnev. The latest is the one staged under Gorbachev and now Yeltsin.[9]

(The strategic update on Russia (Magog) will be addressed in chapter 12. The "Men who would be Gog" will be reviewed in chapter 15.)

The apparent breakup of the Soviet Union, surprisingly, sets the stage for the invasion of Ezekiel 38. But first, let's examine the allies that are to accompany Magog in the ill-fated invasion.

Endnotes:

1. The notorious exploits of Ivan The Terrible are hardly more shocking than the Massacre of St. Bartholemew's Day or the methods of the Roman Catholic Inquisition. See Dave Hunt's *A Woman Rides the Beast*, Harvest House, 1994.

2. *Jerusalem Bible, New English Bible, New American Standard Bible.*

3. *King James, Ryrie's Study Bible, Revised Standard, New American Bible, New International Version.*

4. Riasanovsky, Nicholas V., "The Norman Theory of the Origin of the Russian State," *The Russian Review* 7, 1947, pp 96-110; reprinted in *Readings in Russian History*, ed. S. Harcave, Thomas Y. Crowell, NY, 1962, vol 1, pp 128-138.

5. The Viking, or "Normanist," theory was initiated in the 18th century, by German historians Gottlieb Siegrfied Bayer (1694-1738) and August Ludwig von Schlözer (1735-1809), relying on a 12th century document, *The Primary Russian Chronicle*, which current scholars now consider unreliable.

6. Old Church Slavonic Language, or Old Bulgarian.

7. It is interesting to note that the Czars of Russia, the Kaiser of Germany, and the *qaysars* of the Islamic world, all echo the name of Julius *Caesar* of the Roman Empire.

8. See *Iron Mixed With Clay*, Koinonia House.

9. Don McAlvany, *The McAlvany Intelligence Advisor*, March 1995. P.O. Box 84904, Phoenix AZ 85071.

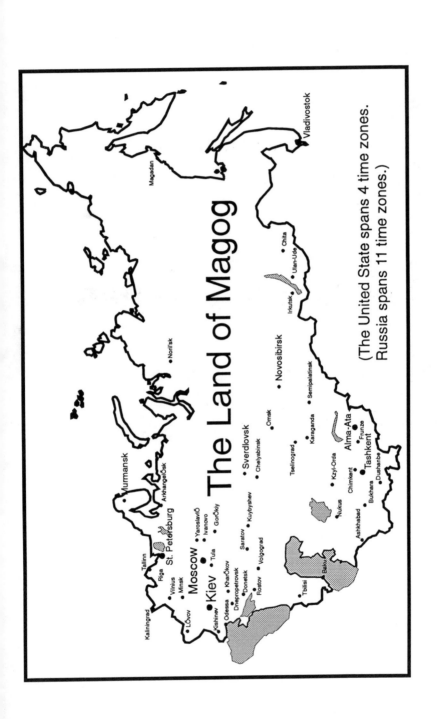

The Land of Magog

Murmansk
Arkhangel0sk
Kaliningrad
Tallinn
Riga
Vilnius
Minsk
LOvov
Kishinev
Odessa
Kharkov
Dnepropetrovsk
Donetsk
Rostov
Volgograd
Tbilisi
Baku
Moscow
Kiev
Tula
GorOkiy
Ivanovo
YaroslavlO
Saratov
Kuybyshev
Norilsk
Sverdlovsk
Chelyabinsk
Omsk
Tselinograd
Kzyl-Orda
Chimkent
Karaganda
Semipalatinsk
Alma-Ata
Frunze
Tashkent
Dushanbe
Bukhara
Ashkhabad
Nukus
Novosibirsk
Magadan
Vladivostok
Irkutsk
Ulan-Ude
Chita
St. Petersburg

(The United State spans 4 time zones.
Russia spans 11 time zones.)

Section III

The Ultimate Jihad

They have openly commited to it.
They have been preparing for it.
They are almost ready.

Chapter 7:

The Allies of Magog

And I will turn thee back, and put hooks into thy jaws, and I will bring thee forth, and all thine army, horses and horsemen, all of them clothed with all sorts of armour, even a great company with bucklers and shields, all of them handling swords:

Persia, Ethiopia, and Libya with them; all of them with shield and helmet:

Gomer, and all his bands; the house of Togarmah of the north quarters, and all his bands: and many people with thee.

Ezekiel 38:4-6

T he invasion by Magog includes a number of specific allies which are listed by their ancient tribal names. Let's review them in more detail.

Persia

The first ally listed is Persia. Those familiar with Biblical text structures will recognize that the first in a list is usually the dominant or most significant one.[1]

The identification of "Persia," (Old Persian, *parsa;* Elamite, *parsin;* Hebrew, פָּרַס) includes the descendants of Elam, the first son of Shem, and is now modern Iran. The name "Persia" is first encountered as *Parsua* in the Assyrian texts of 9th century B.C.[2] The official name of the country became Iran in 1935, as a cognate of *Aryan.*[3]

Elam's descendants are not "Arabs" nor even descendants of Abraham. Abraham's genealogy comes through Arphaxad, not Elam. (The Arabs are the subject of the next chapter.)

Language

The Iranians are Indo-European speaking,[4] and not Arabic speaking like their Muslim neighbors, such as Iraq to the west.

The modern Persian language, although written in Arabic characters, is an Indo-European language related to Sanskrit, Greek, Latin and English. Farsi is derived from Middle Persian (Pahlavi), which was written as a script developed from the Aramaic alphabet and from Old Persian which was written in a cuneiform.[5]

Related language families include: Kurdish (spoken in Turkey, Iraq and Iran); Balochi in the Baluchistan areas of Pakistan and Iran; and Pashto in Afghanistan.

Early History

The Elamites were the rivals of the Mesopotamians in the 3rd and 2nd millennia B.C. Toward the end of the 2nd millennium B.C., Scythian tribes from the steppes of Russia infiltrated Iran and settled in the west. They are recorded by the Assyrians in the 9th century B.C. as the Madai (Medes) and as the Parsua (Persians).

After three decades of subjugation by the invading Scythians from Russia, the Medes became united in the 7th century. They dominated the Persians until the rise of Cyrus, who was half-Median and half-Persian.

The Rise of Cyrus

Cyrus II ("the Great," 559-530 B.C.) was the founder of the Achaemenid Persian Empire that continued for two centuries until the time of Alexander the Great (331 B.C.).

Cyrus' father, Cambyses I (600-559 B.C.), was king of Anshan, a region in eastern Elam. His mother was Mandane, a daughter of Astyages, king of Media (585-550 B.C.).

When Cambyses I died in 559 B.C., Cyrus inherited the throne of Anshan and, after unifying the Persian people, attacked the weak and corrupt Astyages. The Median general Harpagus, whom Astyages had previously wronged, deserted the king and brought his army to the side of the young Cyrus. Astyages was soon captured and the Persians took the capital city of Ecbatana in 550 B.C., without a battle. (This was also to be the result at Babylon 11 years later.)

Cyrus succeeded in welding the Medes and Persians into a unified nation. Moving swiftly to the west, he absorbed all the Median territories as far as the Halys River in Asia Minor. When Croesus, the fabulously wealthy king of Lydia, refused to recognize the sovereignty of Medo-Persia, Cyrus defeated him in battle and took over his empire in 546 B.C. Seven years later, he was ready to launch the great assault against Babylon itself.

The Conquest of Babylon

Babylon was in no position to resist a Medo-Persian invasion in the year 539 B.C. During the preceding fourteen years, Nabonidus the king had not so much as visited the capital city, leaving the administration of the metropolis to his profligate son Belshazzar, to whom he also "entrusted the kingship."[6] Nabonidus further weakened the empire by incurring the displeasure of the powerful Babylonian priesthood.

Toward the end of September, the armies of Cyrus, under the able command of Ugbaru, district governor of Gutium, attacked Opis on the Tigris River and defeated the Babylonians. This gave the Persians control of the vast canal system of Babylon. On October 10, Sippar was taken without a battle and Nabonidus fled. Two days later, on October 12, 539 B.C., Ugbaru's troops were able to enter Babylon *without a battle*.

Herodotus describes how the Persians diverted the River Euphrates into a canal up river so that the water level dropped "to the height of the middle of a man's thigh," which thus rendered the flood defenses useless and enabled the invaders to march through the river bed to enter by night.[7] Cyrus was able to boast that the conquest was almost bloodless with no significant damage to the city.[8] The details of that fateful night, and the famed "handwriting on the wall," are colorfully recorded in Daniel chapter 5.

God's Personal Letter to Cyrus

Daniel (who lived at least until the third year of Cyrus) presented Cyrus with the writings of Isaiah[9] that included a letter, written 150 years earlier, which *was addressed to Cyrus by name*, and highlighted his career and conquest of Babylon.[10] Cyrus was so impressed, he gave orders to release the Jewish captives. The Jews were actually encouraged by Cyrus to return to Jerusalem and to rebuild their temple.[11]

It was a successor, Artaxerxes I (465-423 B.C.) who issued the specific decree concerning the rebuilding of the *walls* of Jerusalem. This decree is the trigger for one of the most remarkable prophecies in the Bible: the famous "Seventy Weeks" of Daniel 9, which will be reviewed in chapter 16.

Persia proper was bounded on the west by Susiana or Elam, on the north by Media, on the south by the Persian Gulf and on the east by Carmania. The peak of Persian history was under the Achaemenid rulers--Cyrus and his successors. They extended the Persian Empire from India on the east to Egypt and Thrace on the west, and included, besides portions of Europe and Africa, the whole of western Asia between the Black Sea, the Caucasus, the Caspian and the Jaxartes on the north, the Arabian desert, the Persian Gulf and the Indian Ocean on the south.

Alexander the Great

The Persians under Darius and Xerxes were defeated by the heroic efforts of the Greeks at Marathon (490 B.C.), at Salamis (480 B.C.) and Plataea and Mycale (479 B.C.).

However, just as Daniel predicted, toward the end of the 4th century, Alexander the Great decisively defeated the Persian forces at Granicus in western Turkey, Issos in southeastern Turkey, and Gaugamela/Arbela in Mesopotamia, and thus established the Greek Empire, pushing all the way to India.

Parthian Empire

After Alexander's death in 323 B.C., Mesopotamia and Persia were inherited by Seleucus, one of his four generals.

This area proved too vast for the Seleucids to control, and ultimately led to the establishment of an independent Persian kingdom by the Parthians around 250 B.C.

During their 500-year history, the Parthians proved to be among the most formidable enemies of the Romans. They ignominiously defeated Crassus at Carrhae (Harran) in 53 B.C. Only Trajan was able to temporarily seize Mesopotamia in 115 A.D.

It was the priestly caste of the Persian Magi, the "king-makers" of the Parthians, that visited Jerusalem in Matthew chapter 2--with cavalry escort--that panicked the city and threatened Herod with a potential border incident.[12]

The Sasanians

A new Persian dynasty, the Sasanians, took control in 226 A.D., and then established Zoroastrianism as the official state religion. The Sasanians were in constant conflict with the late Roman Emperors and the Byzantine rulers.

The Muslim Arabs defeated the Sasanians at Ctesiphon in 637 and annexed Persia to the Arab Empire in 642. (The Iranians, unlike most Muslims, are Shi'ites. This will be reviewed in chapter 9.)

After 800 A.D., Iran was ruled, in turn, by a rapid succession of competing dynasties such as the Tahirids, the Samanids, the Saffarids, the Zizarids, the Buyids, and the Ghaznavids. Iran was then invaded by the Seljuk Turks (11th-12th centuries), the Mongols (13th-14th centuries), the Tatars (14th-15th centuries), the Safavids (16th-18th centuries), the Zends (18th century), and the Qajars (19th-early 20th centuries).

Modern Iran

In 1925 General Reza Khan led a revolt and became the Shahanshah ("King of Kings"). As he was sympathetic to the Germans, the British forced him to abdicate in 1941 in favor of his son Reza Shah Pahlavi.

The name *Iran* was instituted in 1935 by Reza Shah Pahlavi. It is derived from the term in the Avesta, *airyana;* Middle Iranian, *'ry'n,* "Aryan;" New Persian, *Iran.*

Using their oil revenues, Shah Pahlavi dramatically westernized and modernized Iran's industry and armed forces. In 1971, Iran celebrated the nation's 2500th anniversary with unprecedented pomp and pageantry at Persepolis. Royal guests from 70 countries watched 6,000 marchers representing ten dynasties of Persian history pass in review.

Less than a decade later, the popular revolution inspired by Ayatollah Khomeini forced the Shah into exile on January 16, 1979. The Islamic revolution resulted in the persecution of both Jews and Christians, and the abandonment of further archaeological and cultural investigations of Iran's proud past.[13]

Iran (Persia) is the leading ally in Ezekiel's list and it is interesting that Iran is now emerging as the principal leader in the rise of "Islamic Fundamentalism," and is attempting to coalesce the Shi'ite influence among the former southern Soviet Republics known as Central Asia: Kazakhstan, Turkmenistan, Tadzhikistan, Uzbekistan, and Kirgyzstan (formerly Kirghizia).

These former Soviet Republics may prove to be the "hooks in the jaws" as will be highlighted later in this report.

Cush

The next ally in Ezekiel's list is Cush, (Hebrew, כוּשׁ; LXX[14], Χους, and Αἰθιοπία), and refers to a land lying to the south of Egypt, usually translated in many English Bibles as "Ethiopia."[15]

Originally Cush referred to a piece of territory lying between the second and third cataracts of the Nile. Later it came to refer to a broader area known as Nubia. In broad, connotative usage, it is generally viewed as embracing "Black Africa."

As in all of the allies of Magog, we find that, here too, there is a dominance of Islam. The rapid growth of Islam will be discussed in Chapter 9.

Strategic Materials

There are a dozen strategic materials--essential to the modern military and industrial world--which are available in only two regions: Russia and Africa.

And not just in South Africa. Take Zaire, for instance: its resources include 95% of the world's known reserves of chromium, 52% of its cobalt, 53% of its manganese, 64% of its vanadium and 86% of its platinum group of metals[16] No wonder Zaire is called "The Persian Gulf of Minerals."

critical materials. Russia is uniquely endowed, importing only three important minerals: bauxite (used to make aluminum), barium, and flouride. They are self-sufficient in 26 of the 36 minerals considered essential for an industrial society.

Together with South Africa, the Russians control over 90% of the world's supply of platinum, over 94% of the world's supply of manganese, over 90 % of the chrome, over 95% of the vanadium.

With the rise of Mandela, and his KGB sidekick Joe Slovo, the strategic significance of these materials are of grave concern to the strategists of the West. With Mandela as a role model, and the continuing growth of Islam among the turbulent countries of the "Dark Continent," Cush may prove to be a larger factor than many suppose.

Phut

The next ally of Magog in Ezekiel 38 is Phut (Hebrew, פוּט; LXX, Φουδ). Phut was the third son of Ham. Josephus identifies him as the founder of Libya whose inhabitants were called Putites.[17]

In the connotative sense, Phut (or Put) is associated with North Africa, populated by the Berbers and tribes distinct from Cush, and, thus, reaches from Libya to Mauritania and the Mahgreb: Algeria, Tunisia, and Morocco.

(When I was a consultant to Sonotrach, the nationalized oil industry of Algeria, we had an introduction to the folk legends of the Mahgreb including the matriarchical society of the

Tuajari's of the deep Sahara. The cultural diversity in various parts of the world is astonishing.)

The militaristic rhetoric of Algeria quieted down measurably when Israel gained fighter jets with a range that included Algeria, but now the militant Muslim extremists are gathering their forces. The rise of Islam in Algeria is frequently in the news and we note that despite the government's crackdowns, the Islamic terrorism continues its attempt to take over the government. In recent months this terrorism is even being carried into France.

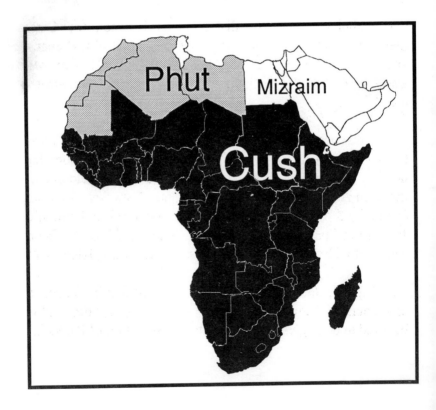

Gomer

Another of Magog's allies is Gomer. In the Babylonian Talmud[18] the Biblical Gomer, the father of Ashkenaz, is rendered "Germania."[19]

Gomer[20] is also associated with the people referred to in nonbiblical sources as the Cimmerians (Akkadian: *Gimmiraia*, Greek: *Kimmerioi*),[21] who eventually established themselves in the Rhine and Danube valleys. (The prehistory of the Cimmerians was discussed in Chapter 3.)

Although Assyrians distinguished between the Cimmerians and the Scythians, later texts of the Neo-Babylonians and Persians (6th - 5th century B.C.) use the term *Gimmiraia* also for *Scythians*.[22] Josephus[23] anachronistically indentified the "Gomarites" with the Celtic Galatians.[24]

Ashkenaz was a son of Gomer.[25] In Old Testament times, the Ashkenazim and Sepharadim represented populations far northeast and northwest of Israel. (By a curious development, the term Ashkenaz has come to designate Jews from Europe, originally those in the Rhine Valley, as opposed to Sephardic Jews from Spain and North Africa. The word has also been confused with the Akkadian name for the Scythians, Ishkuza.)[26]

Riphath, another son of Gomer, is identified by Josephus as associated with the Paplagonians. (Strangely, "Europe" is believed to be linguistically linked to a designation of Riphath.)

Togarmah

Another ally listed in Ezekiel 38 is Togarmah, another son of Gomer. The Assyrians called them Til-Garimmu, a name derived from the Hittite city Tegarama and carried into classical times as Gauraema (modern Gürün), 70 miles west of Malayta. The city was destroyed by Sennacherib in 695 B.C.[27] Josephus refers to them as the Phrygians.

The Armenians still refer to themselves as "The House of Togarmah" even to this day, although they are only one of the Turkic people descending from these ancient tribes.[28] The tribal associations also appear to include Turkey and Turkestan.

The foundations of Armenia were laid in the 6th century B.C. on the ruins of the ancient kingdom of Urartu when it was overrun by the Scythians and Cimmerians in the wake of the conquest of Urartu's powerful ally Assyria by Babylon. Armenia became the focus of Roman and Parthian rivalry from about 66 B.C. to the 3rd century.

Meshech

Meshech and Tubal are also prominent in the opening verses of Ezekiel 38. Meshech was the sixth son of Japheth, the son of Noah. He is identified with the ancient *Mushki* of the Assyrians and the *Muschoi* of the classical Greek writers. The Assyrian inscriptions describe them as inhabiting Phrygia in northern Anatolia (modern Turkey).

The Mushki appear after the collapse of the Hittite Empire in the texts of Tiglath-pileser I (1115-1077 B.C.) who encountered 20,000 of them in the region of Kadmuhu in the Upper

Tigris.[29] Ashurnasirpal II (883-859 B.C.) later received tribute from the Mushki, whose capital was at Mazaca (classical Caesarea, modern Kaysweri) in eastern Turkey.[30]

Herodotus identifies the Mushki with the mountains southeast of the Black Sea, the northeast part of modern Turkey. Josephus also identifies the descendants of Meshech as dwelling in eastern Turkey.

Some also link the *Muschkoi* with *Mushkovi*, the ancient name for Russia.

Tubal

Tubal was the 5th son of Japheth and a brother of M-eshech. 9th century B.C. Assyrian inscriptions refer to Tabal, just west of Meshech in eastern Anatolia. Geographically neighbors, they became allies against the Assyrians in 713 B.C.[31] The classical Greek writers called them the Tibareni. Herodotus also places them both along the southeastern shores of the Black Sea. Some associate Tubal with naming of Tobolsk of Russia.

Tabal, the region between Mazaca and the Taurus Mountains to the south, was attacked in 836 B.C. by Shalmaneser III.[32] Tiglath-pileser III assaulted Tabal in 732 B.C. when its king did not present the expected tribute.[33] An inscription of Tiglath-pileser III discovered by L. D. Levine in Iran in 1967 gives the name of the king of Tabal as Wassurme, a ruler whose own inscriptions have been discovered around Kayseri.[34] Sargon II boasted of his success in suppressing Tabal in 713 B.C., after it had signed a treaty with Urartu, Assyria's enemy.[35]

Some of the Mushki may eventually have migrated northward and apparently gave their name to Moscow (and Tubal to the Tibereni and Tobolsk), but this tradition is not free of controversy.[36] It is important to note that our identification of Magog with Russia is *not* on the basis of these possible linquistic links, but on contemporary documents of the period.

Central Asia

The breakup of the Soviet Union also released the Central Asian Republics (Kazakhstan, Turkmenistan, Uzbekistan, Tadzhikistan, and Kyrgyzstan) to join their Islamic brethren in their fanatical effort to destroy Israel.

These five independent republics are Islamic, have nuclear weapons, and may well prove to be the "hooks in the jaw" to draw Magog directly into this ill-fated invasion of Israel.

Puzzling Omissions

Some of the striking aspects of the Ezekiel passage are the elements that are conspicuous by their *omission.* Students of Biblical prophecy may be surprised to note the absence of any mention of *Mizraim* (Egypt), who is a key player as the "King of the South" in the Armageddon passages, specifically, Daniel 11.

Another surprising omission is the absence of any mention of Babylon or Iraq. This is also a prominent aspect of the climactic end-time passages.[37]

A further puzzling omission is any reference to the Coming World Leader (the "Antichrist"), unless one assumes that "Gog" is a reference to him. More will be said of the possible leadership persons in Chapter 15.

These omissions will influence our views on the timing of the invasion, as discussed in Chapter 17.

Summary

All of the allies of Magog (Russia) are reasonably well identified and all of them are Muslim. Their intense hatred of, as well as their commitment to destroy, Israel unites them in a common cause. To fully understand the dynamics behind today's (and tomorrow's) headlines, we need to understand the real nature of Islam which is the subject of chapter 9.

The present lineup of allies with Magog makes Ezekiel 38 and 39 appear more imminent with each issue of our daily newspaper.

The more one examines current intelligence estimates, the more it would seem that this famed invasion which Ezekiel describes *could happen at any time.*

Strategic updates on each of the major players will be reviewed in Section IV.

Endnotes:

1.   Genesis 14:1 is an example. The king of Babylon is mentioned first; while he was junior player at the time, Babylon emerges as central to the Biblical narrative.

2.   Yamauchi, Edwin, *Persia and the Bible*, p.19.

3.   See V.G. Childe, *The Aryans: A Story of Indo-European Origins,* Knopf, New York, 1926; also Leon Poliakov, *The Aryan Myth*, Sussex University Press, London, 1974.

4.   The original home of the Indo-Europeans was southwest Russia. See M. Gimbutas, "The Indo-Europeans: Archaeological Problems," American Anthropologist 65 (1963), p. 815-36; R. N. Frye, *The History of Ancient Iran,* C. H. Beckische, Munich, 1984, pp. 45, 47.

5.   R.G. Kent, *Old Persian*, American Oriental Society, New Haven, 1953.

6.   "Verse Account of Nabonidus," Pritchard, *Ancient Near Eastern Texts,* 313.

7.   Herodotus 1.191.

8.   The famous Steele of Cyrus: "...without any battle, he entered the town, sparing any calamity...I returned to sacred cities on the other side of the Tigris, the sanctuaries of which have been ruins for a long time...and established for them permanent sanctuaries. I also gathered all their former inhabitants and returned to them their habitations."

9.   Josephus, Antiq. XI, i.2.

10.   Isaiah 44:27 - 45:7.

11.   2 Chronicles 36:22; Ezra 1:1-4.

12.   See *The Christmas Story: What Really Happened*, Koinonia House, for some surprising background.

13.   The U.S. severed ties with Iran in 1979, after the U.S. Embassy was stormed in Tehran; 52 hostages were freed after 444 days in captivity.

14.   LXX is the universal abbreviation of the Septuagint translation of the Old Testament into Greek, completed 270 B.C.

15.   The exception is Isaiah 11:11 and II Samuel 18:21-23 where it is *Cushi*. Sometimes the word Cush is used to refer to the land (Isaiah 11:11; 18:1; Zephaniah 1:1; Esther 1:1.) Sometimes the reference is to the people as in Isaiah 20:5; Jeremiah 46:9; and Ezekiel 38:5.

16.   Platinum, palladium, iridium, rhodium, and others.

17. Antiquities I 6.2.

18. Yoma 10a.

19. See Ashkenaz, *Encyclopedia Judaica*, Jerusalem, 1971, vol 1, pp. 720-722.

20. Genesis 10:2-3; Ezekiel 38:6.

21. S. Parpola, *Neo-Assyrian Toponyms*, Butzon and Bercker, Kavelaer, West Germany, 1970, pp. 132-134.; cf also, J. N. Postgate's review of S. Parpola, ed. Neo-Assyrian Letters from the Kuyunjik Collection, in *Journal of Semitic Studies*, 25, 1980, p. 241.

22. Later writers such as Strabo (1.3.21) seem to use the term Cimmerian interchangeably with Scythian.

23. *Antiquities*, 1.123.

24. Defended by A.C. Custance, *Noah's Three Sons*, Zondervan, Grand Rapids, 1975, p. 83.

25. Genesis 10:3; I Chronicles 1:6; and Jeremiah 51:27.

26. S. Parpola, *Neo-Assyrian Toponyms*, Butzon and Bercker, Kevelaer, West Germany, 1970, p. 178.

27. Cf. Cogan and Tadmor, "Gyges", pp. 80-81.

28. The Turkic peoples are historically and linguistically linked with T'uchüeh, the name given by the Chinese to the nomad peoples who founded an empire stretching from Mongolia and the northern frontier of China to the Black Sea. The name originated from that of one of the khans of the Golden Horde who embraced Islam. They were all Muslim.

29. A. K. Grayson, *Assyrian Royal Inscriptions*, O. Harrassowitz, Wiesbaden, 1976, vol 2, pp. 6-7.

30. Luckenbill, *Ancient Records*, vol 1, pp. 138-144.

31. M. Jastrow, "Notes on Meshek and Tubal," *American Journal of Semitic Languages* 13 (1996-1897) p. 217; A. T. Olmstead, "The Assyrians in Asia Minor," in *Anatolian Studies*, ed. W. H. Buckler, Manchester University, Manchester, 1923, pp. 283-296; idem, *History of Assyria*, University of Chicago, Chicago, 1923, pp. 143-144, 221-228, 266-267; A H. Sayce, "The Early Geography of South-Eastern Asia Minor," *Journal of Hellenic Studies*, 43, 1923, pp. 44-49; G. A. Wainwright, "Tabal, Tibareni, Tebarani," *Orietalistische Literaturzeitung* 39, 1936,pp. 479-481; P. Naster, *L'Asie Mineure et l'Assyrie*, Bureaux du Museon, Louvain, 1938; E. Dhorme, "Les peuples issus de Japhet d'apres le chapitre X de la Genese," *Recueil Edouard dhorme*, Imprimerie Nationale, Paris, 1951, pp. 167-189; E. Cavignac, "Mushki et Phrygiens," *Journal Asiatique* 241, 1953, pp. 139-143; R. D. Barnett,

       Phrygia and the Peoples of Anatolia in the Iron Age, Cambridge University, Cambridge, 1967; E.S. Edwards, et al, ed., *Cambridge Ancient History,* 1975, vol 2, ch 30, pp. 417-442.

32.   Naster, *L'Asie Mineure,* pp.7ff.

33.   D. J. Wiseman, "A Fragmentary Inscription of Tiglath-pileser III from Nimrud," *Iraq* 18, 1956, p. 122.

34.   L.D. Levine, *Two Neo-Assyrian Stelae from Iran,* Royal Ontario Museum, Toronto, 1972, pp. 11ff.19. M. Weippert, "Menahem von Israel und seine Zeitgenossen in einer Steleninschrift des assyrischen Konigs Tiglath-pileser III. us dem Iran", *Zeitschrift des Deutschen Palastina-Vereins* 89, 1973, p. 30.

35.   Luckenbill, *Ancient Records,* vol 2, pp. 12,21-23,46-48; cf. Cogan and Tadmor, "Gyges", pp. 80-81.

36.   R. H. Alexander, "A Fresh Look at Ezekiel 38 and 39," *Journal of the Evangelical Theological Society,* 17, 1974, pp. 161-162; idem, *Ezekiel,* Moody, Chicago, 1976, p. 122; E. M. Blaiklock, *Zondervan Pictorial Bible Atlas,* Zondervan, Grand Rapids, 1969, p. 45; J. J. Davis, *Paradise to Prison,* Baker, Grand Rapids, 1975, pp. 138-139; C. L. Feinberg, *The Prophecy of Ezekiel,* Moody, Chicago, 1969, p. 220; J. B. Payne, *Enclyopedia of Bible Prophecy, the Complete Guide to Scriptural Predictions and Their Fulfillment,* Harper and Row, NY, 1973, p. 367; J. B. Taylor, *Ezekiel,* Tyndale, London, 1969, p. 244; E. Yamauchi, "Meshek, Tubal and company," *Journal of the Evangelical Theological Society,* 19, 1976, pp. 239-247.

37.   Isaiah 13,14; Jeremiah 50, 51.

Chapter 8:

Where are the Arabs?

And the angel of the Lord said unto her, I will multiply thy seed exceedingly, that it shall not be numbered for multitude.

And the angel of the Lord said unto her, Behold, thou art with child, and shalt bear a son, and shalt call his name Ishmael; because the Lord hath heard thy affliction.

And he will be a wild man; his hand will be against every man, and every man's hand against him; and he shall dwell in the presence of all his brethren.

Genesis 16:10-12

The newspapers and television media are constantly referring to the "Arabs." Who are they? What does this term include and exclude? It is interesting how this term reveals the widespread illiteracy about the Middle East.

The Ishmael Myths

The Arabs lay claim to Palestine as the alleged descendants of Abraham through Ishmael, born to him by Hagar, Sarah's handmaid.[1] It was predicted that he would be "A wild donkey of a man, and his hand will be against everyone, and everyone's hand against him, and he will dwell (settle, encamp) in the presence ("in the face") of his brothers."[2]

The Bible makes it clear, however, that Isaac, not Ishmael, is the heir to the promise of the land of Canaan which God committed to Abraham.[3] The Jews are clearly the descendants of Abraham through his son, Isaac, by his wife, Sarah.

Isaac is confirmed as the legitimate heir in the Torah, the New Testament--even in the Koran.[4] Parts of the Koran honor

the Torah as true.[5] The Koran even testifies that the Jews, the
descendants of Israel (Jacob), and not the Arabs, are the
legitimate heirs to the promised land.[6] (There are many
inconsistencies and self-contradictions in the Koran.[7])

Even if Ishmael *were* the legitimate heir, it would be of
little use to the "Arab" cause. Neither they, nor anyone else,
can trace their ancestry back to Ishmael.[8] The Arabs actually
descended from numerous nomadic tribes of uncertain origin.
What about all the Akkadians, Sumerians, Assyrians, Babylonians, Persians, Egyptians, Hittites, etc. that lived before,
during, and after Abraham?[9]

While no one disputes that Ishmael was fathered by
Abraham, there were many other descendants who became so
many different nations. After the death of Sarah, he married
Keturah, by whom he had six more sons.[10] Isaac also had two
sons, Esau and Jacob. Esau despised his inheritance and sold
it to Jacob, who was later renamed Israel and confirmed in the
covenant.[11]

To insist that an "Arab" is a descendant of Ishmael would
be to deny that a Bedouin is an Arab: they are descendants from
Keturah, not from Hagar, the mother of Ishmael.

There is no indication that Ishmael's descendants attempted to keep themselves from intermarrying with the
peoples around them as the Jews did. There was no such
command to any other of Abraham's descendants.

The descendants of Keturah, Esau and Ishmael are
unidentifiable today. Intermarriage occurred in the very next
generation for there was no reason for them not to have done

so.[12]   The Midianite nation was one result of Abraham's marriage to Keturah and these distant relatives became implacable enemies of Israel. They became so mixed by marriage with the descendants of Ishmael that they were also called Ishmaelites.[13]

The Cave of Machpelah, also known as the Cave of Patriarchs, in Hebron, Israel, is where Abraham, Sarah, Isaac, Rebecca, Jacob and Leah are buried.[14] Ishmael is not. Ishmael's burial site is somewhere in a region described as "from Havilah unto Shur, that is before Egypt, as thou goest toward Assyria."[15]

Jordan

Any discussion of the "Arabs" must also bring into focus the Hashemite Kingdom of Jordan, a European creation of 1946.

During World War I, the British and the Allies fought the Ottoman Turks as well as the Germans. The area east of the Jordan River, known in the Bible as Moab and Gilead, had been populated by unaffiliated Arabic Bedouin tribes. Major T.E. Lawrence organized the "Arab Revolt" to assist against the Turks. General Allenby was victorious in Middle East, and the League of Nations awarded the British "Mandate" on April 25, 1920, which endured until the State of Israel was declared on May 14, 1948.

In 1921, the son of Sharif Hussein of Mecca in Arabia, an aggressive young man named Abdallah, moved in with his troops, to the land east of Jordan. The British Colonial Secretary, Winston Churchill, found it expedient to recognize

Abdallah as the emir (chieftain) of "Trans-Jordan," an invention for the occasion. Abdallah then consolidated his control with his British-trained "Arab Legion."

After the war, in 1946, Abdallah was crowned King of Transjordan. His grandson, Hussein, is the current king.

Jordan joined in on the attack on Israel during its War of Independence in 1948, and the "Arab Legion" successfully fought the Haganah and held the "West Bank." However, again joining Egypt in the famed Six Day War, they lost it in 1967.

It is interesting that the Bible predicts that this region-- Edom, Moab and Ammon--will be the only regions which escape the grasp of the Coming World Leader (commonly referred to as the Antichrist).[16] Some speculate that this is to allow a faithful remnant to flee to Petra in Jordan during the final attack on Jerusalem at Armageddon.[17]

The Peace Treaty between Jordan and Israel, effective November 1, 1994, and ending a state of war which has lasted nearly 50 years, may prove to be setting the stage for this final scene.

The Confusion Broadens

If you lump together Egypt, Iraq, Libya, Syria, Iran and Turkey into a single group, it may come as a surprise to discover that there isn't an "Arab" among them! In fact, many of these hate the Arabs.

Noah repopulated the earth after the flood through his three sons: Ham, Shem and Japheth.

Egypt originally descended from Mizraim, a son of Ham.[18] Iraq is the current term for the plain of Shinar, Babylon, and the first world empire established by Nimrod, the son of Cush, also a son of Ham.[19] Libya originally descended from Phut, another son of Ham.[20]

Syria derives from Aram, one of the five sons of Shem.[21] Iran (Persia) descends from Elam, another son of Shem[22] (although some ethnologists regard them as non-Semitic Caucasians). Notice that while both Aram and Elam are descendants of Shem, Abraham descends from Arphaxad, a different son of Shem.[23]

Turkey (Meshech and Tubal) originally descended from Japheth, along with the Greeks.[24]

Here we have the descendants from each of the three sons of Noah: Ham, Shem, and Japheth, all lumped into one group. These have no common genealogy except for Noah, which we all have in common.

The centuries of intermarriage among all of these people has rendered the ethnic lines increasingly indistinct. Using the term "Arab" *denotatively* would imply an inhabitant of the Arabian peninsula.

Sheba

There are several Sheba's in the Bible. One of them was a descendant of Ham. Sheba's descendants are believed to have settled on the shores of the Persian Gulf.[25]

Another Sheba was a son of Joktan of the family of Shem, whose descendants have been traced to southern Arabia.[26]

A grandson of Abraham named Sheba was a son of Jokshan, who was a son of Abraham by Keturah. Sheba and his descendants probably lived in Edom or northern Arabia.[27]

Sheba is also a mountainous country in southwest Arabia,[28] identified as the land of "the queen of the South"[29] who came to investigate Solomon's fame and wisdom. The Queen of Sheba's visit to Solomon may have also been motivated by her interest in trade and in the unhindered movement of her caravans into the large territory under Solomon's control.

Dedan

Dedan is a name of two men and a geographical region in the Bible. One is a descendant of Cush,[30] the other was a son of Jokshan, thus a grandson of Abraham and Keturah.[31] It is also a district near Edom and the Dead Sea.[32]

Both Sheba and Dedan are identified with the Arabian Peninsula, and we will encounter these in Ezekiel 38 as they cower nervously on the sidelines during the Magog invasion. When we examine the current intelligence horizon, we'll also understand why.

It is the use of the term "Arab" *connotatively* that contributes to the confusion. The media--and common usage, now--collectively refers to any of the enemies of Israel as "the Arabs." Although coming from highly diverse ethnic backgrounds, what unites these peoples is their *commitment to*

Islam, and, thus, their common hatred of "The People of the Book."

To understand the increasing tensions emerging on our horizon, it is essential to understand the origin, the goals, and the agenda of Islam. This will be the focus of the next chapter.

We are being drawn into the Ultimate Jihad--and we all need to understand what we are up against.

Endnotes:

1. Genesis 16:1ff.

2. Genesis 16:10-12; 17:20-21; 21:8-21; 25:9, 12-18.

3. Land Grant: Genesis 15:7-8, 13-16; 17:8; Deuteronomy 28-30; Jerermiah 30-31; Ezekiel 36.
    Boundaries: Genesis 15:18-21; Exodus 23:24-31; Numbers 34:1-14; Joshua 1:3; Ezekiel 47:13ff. From the "River of Egypt" to the Euphrates: from eastern Egypt, past Damascus, all the way into western Iraq.

4. Dave Hunt, *A Cup of Trembling*, p.79.

5. Surah 3:3, 48, 65, 93; 5:43ff, 66, 68, 61:6 et al.

6. Surah 5:20, 21.

7. See Robert Morey, *The Islamic Invasion*, Harvest House 1992; Dave Hunt, *A Cup of Trembling*; Harvest House 1995; et al. Also, a briefing package, *The Sword of Allah*, Koinonia House.

8. John McClintock and James Strong, *Cyclopedia of Biblical, Theological, and Ecclesiastical Literature*, Baker Book House, Grand Rapids MI, 1981 reprint. I:339; Gibb, Levi-Provencial, Schacht, eds, *The Encyclopedia of Islam*, J. Brill, Leiden, 1913, I:543-47; Thomas Hughes, *A Dictionary of Islam*, Allen & Co., London, 1885; pp.18ff.

9. Robert Morey, *The Islamic Invasion*, Harvest House, 1992, p.24.

10. Genesis 25:1-4.

11. Genesis 32:28.

12. Genesis 25:12-18; 28:9; et al.

13. Judges 8:1,24.

14. Genesis 23:19; 25:10; 49:31; 50:13,14.

15. Genesis 25:18.

16. Daniel 11:41.

17. It is here at Petra (Bosra) that the Lord is seen returning to fight for them. Isaiah 63.

18. Genesis 10:6, 13,14; 1 Chronicles 1:8, 11, 12.

19. Genesis 10:8, 9, 10.

20. Genesis 10:6; 1 Chronicles 1:18.

21. Genesis 10:22,23; 1 Chronicles 1:17; Numbers 23:7; 2 Samuel 15:8; Hosea 12:12.

22. Genesis 10:22; 1 Chronicles 1:17.

23. 1 Chronicles 1:17-27.

24. Genesis 10:12.

25. Genesis 10:7.

26. Genesis 10:28.

27. Genesis 25:3.

28. 1 Kings 10:1-13.

29. Luke 11:31.

30. Genesis 10:7-1; 1 Chronicles 1:9.

31. Genesis 25:3; 1 Chronicles 1:32.

32. Jerermiah 25:23; Ezekiel 25:13; 27:15.

Chapter 9:

The Sword of Allah

Fight and slay the pagans (infidels) wherever ye find them, and seize them, beleaguer them, and lie in wait for them in every stratagem of war.

Koran, Sura 9:5

"Believers (Muslims), take neither Jews nor Christians to be your friends: they are friends with one another. Whoever of you seeks their friendship shall become one of their number, and God does not guide (those Jewish and Christian) wrongdoers."

Koran, Sura 5:51-5:74

We do not despise Muslims; but we must fear the implications of their occultic religion. Their agenda can no longer be ignored: they now believe they have the resources (their oil revenues and, now, nuclear weapons) to disconnect the Middle East from the Judeo-Christian order of the West.

And their "*jihad*" is not just against the Jews, it is also directed against the entire non-Muslim world. The world of Islam divides the entire universe into only two parts:

Dar Al Islam: the domain of the faithful (to Islam);

Dar Al Harb: those with whom they are at war until Judgement Day. (Not just the Jews: *all non-Muslims*!)

The goal of Islam is the subjugation of the entire world--by the sword if necessary. The present tenet of Islam is that "it has replaced Marxism as the ideology of the future and that it now has the resources to overthrow the Judeo-Christian world order of the West."

Spectacular Growth

Islam commands almost 1.5 *billion* adherents, and is the fastest growing religion on the Planet Earth. Islam is clearly the greatest challenge to Christianity--and the free world--in the 90's.

There are more Muslims than evangelical Christians in Britain; more than 1.000 churches have been converted to mosques in the U.K.

There are more Muslims than Jews in North America. There are now more than 1,100 mosques in the U.S.

It may come as a surprise to discover that Islam *did not begin with Muhammad.*

Pre-Islamic Arabia

When Abraham was called out of the Ur of the Chaldees,[1] the main religion of the region was the worship of the Moon-god which would ultimately become the supreme deity of the entire Babylonian empire.

The Sabeans' Religion

Before the advent of Muhammad, the Sabeans in Arabia were committed to an astral religion, worshiping heavenly bodies. The moon was viewed as a male deity; the sun, a female deity; the stars were viewed as their offspring.

It was from this background that the lunar calendar resulted. Fasting was, and still is, done from crescent moon to crescent moon.

One of the names for the Moon-god was "Sin." ("Sin Ech-erib," the famed Assyrian king, meant "Sin multiplies his brothers").[2] "Sin" was elevated to the top of the Babylonian pantheon by Nabu-na'id (Nabodnidus) in an effort to make the Babylonian religion more acceptable to their subjects like the Arabians and the Aramaeans, who esteemed the moon god, and had difficulty identifying with Marduk, the supreme Babylonian deity associated primarily with the city of Babylon.

Sin, "The Controller of the Night," had the crescent moon as its emblem, and the lunar-based calendar, which later became the primary religious symbols of Islam. The Moon-god was worshiped in Arabia as Al-Ilah, later simplified to Allah. Allah was the "Lord of the Ka'aba" ("cube"), the center of pagan worship, ruling over 360 idols. Lucrative trade routes resulted. Mecca became the center of all pagan religions of Arabia.

It is interesting to note that Jericho, the capital of the Amorites and the first battle in Joshua's conquest of Canaan, was named after the Moon-god: Beth-Yerah, "House (Temple) of the Moon God."

It was required--long before Muhammad--to bow and pray toward Mecca. Pilgrimages there were required; the Ka'aba, site of a protective black stone, was circled seven times, kissed, and then the pilgrims would run to Wadi Mina to throw stones at the Devil. These pagan rituals are still practiced in Islam today.

Pagans worshiped toward Mecca because that's where their idols were located. This pagan worship was very widespread, which explains the rapid acceptance of Muhammad's religion.

The Life of Muhammad

The Quraysh tribe (into which Muhammad was born) was *previously* devoted to Allah, the moon god. Muhammad's father was named Abd-Allah. His Uncle, Obied-Allah. His mother, Aminah, was also involved in the occult.[3]

We won't dwell on the numerous inconsistencies, self-contradictions, and self-serving rulings of convenience, involved with Muhammad and the Koran. But as one example, the Koran forbids more than 4 wives;[4] Muhammad had 16 wives, 2 concubines, and 4 others.[5]

Islam is simply their previous heathenism in a monotheistic form. Their occultic beliefs in jinns (genies, fairies), spells, magic stones, fetishes and other animistic beliefs are still practiced in Islam today.[6] These, of course, are forbidden by God in the Bible.[7]

Archaeological and linguistic work done since the latter part of the 19th century has discovered overwhelming evidence that Muhammad constructed his religion and the Koran from preexisting material in Arabian culture. Particular attention should be paid to the pioneering work of Julius Welhausen, Theordor Noldeke, Joseph Halevvy, Edward Glaser, William F. Albright, Frank P. Albright, Richard Bell, J. Arberry, Wendell Phillips, W. Montgomery Watt, Alfred Guillaume, and Arthur Jeffery.[8]

The Nature of Islam

Islam is a legacy of hate, born of deception, weaned on violence.

Islam means "Submission." Originally, however, it referred to that strength which characterized a desert warrior who, even when faced with impossible odds, would fight to the death for his tribe.[9]

Al-Ilah became Allah, Arabic for "*the* god." It is a pre-Islamic name, corresponding to the Babylonian Bel, the Moon-god, symbolized by the crescent moon.[10]

The Koran

The Koran is an amalgam of Hinduism, Buddhism, Mythraism, Greek mystery religions, as well as elements selected from Judaism and Christianity. The order is confused, with self-contradictions.

Violence is commanded:

Fight and slay the pagans (infidels) wherever ye find them, and seize them, beleaguer them, and lie in wait for them in every stratagem of war.   Sura 9:5

If Islam is resisted?

Their punishment is . . . execution, or crucifixion, or the cutting off of hands and feet from the opposite sides, or exile from the land.   Sura 5:33

Al Tawbah (The Repentence): *"Prophet, make war on unbelievers and hypocrites, and deal rigorously with them."*

Sura 9:73

Al Anfal (The Spoils): *"Let not the unbelievers think they will ever get away.   They have not the power to do so.   Muster against them all the men and cavalry at your command, so that you may strike terror into the enemy of God and your enemy . . . Prophet, (Muhammad) rouse the faithful to arms! If they (the non-Muslims) incline to peace (accept Islam) make peace with them."*   Sura 8:59

Al Maidah (The Table): *"If they reject your judgement, know that it is Allah's wish to scourge them for their sins."*

Sura 5:49

Perfect Arabic is claimed in 12:2; 13:37; 41:41,44. There are, however, over 100 aberrations,[11] such as 2:177,192; 3:59; 4:162; 5:69; 7:160; 13:28; 20:66; 63:10, etc.

Freedom from error is claimed in Sura 85:21,22. It also claims to be consistent with the Bible.   Yet Sura 7:51 and 10:3 claim six days of creation; Sura 41, eight days of creation; Sura 32-48 disagrees with Genesis 7.

There are also numerous errors concerning Abraham: his father's name was not Azar (6:74); he never lived in Mecca[12] (14:37); he did not sacrifice Ishmael (37:100-112); had eight sons, not two; three wives, not two; he did not build the Ka'aba (2:125-127); was not thrown into a fire by Nimrod (21:68,69; 9:69), etc.

There are also numerous chronological errors. The Flood did not occur in Moses' day (Sura 7:136 vs. 7:59ff.)[13]

It is helpful to realize that the Bible was not available in Arabic in Muhammad's day. It was not translated into Arabic until the 9th century.

The Nature of Allah

Is "Allah" equivalent to the God of the Old Testament? Any new revelation must agree with what is already established as God's Word.[14]

The Islamic Allah is unknowable, impersonal, capricious (thus, untrustworthy). The God of the Old Testament is immutable, unchanging, and makes and keeps His covenants and promises.

There are some important contrasts between Muhammad and Jesus Christ. Muhammad was not sinless: Sura 40:55. Nor did he ever perform a single miracle: Sura 17:91-95. He did not die for anyone. Also, no personal relationship is possible: Muhammed is dead.

Not Color-Blind

It's amazing to notice how the American blacks have been widely deceived. Islam claims that only people with white faces will be saved; people with black faces will be damned: Sura 3:106, 107. The Bible states that all are equal in God's sight.[15]

Arab Muslims were enslaving black Africans long before Westerners.

Anti-Judaism

Islam is, of course, conspicuously anti-Jewish.[16] Al Maidah (The Table):

"Believers (Muslims), take neither Jews nor Christians to be your friends: they are friends with one another. Whoever of you seeks their friendship shall become one of their number, and God does not guide (those Jewish and Christian) wrongdoers."   Sura 5:51-5:74

"Say, 'People of the Book' (Jews), is it not that you hate us (Ishamelite Muslims), only because we believe in God, and in what has been revealed to others, and because most of you (Jews) are evil-doers?"   Sura 5:57

Islamic Eschatology

In Islamic eschatology, *Al Dajjal* is the "Antichrist" of Islam. *Al Mahdi* is their expected one, the messianic, miracle-working figure of Islam. (Could he be the false prophet of Revelation 13?)

The Bible predicts a coming world leader that will find acceptance among the Jews.[17] Paul also tells us that he will "exalt himself above all that is called God or that is worshiped."[18] This would seem to imply that he will, somehow, also gain acceptance to the Muslims. (This coming world leader will be discussed further in chapter 16.)

The Shi'ite sect of Islam looks to Muhammad bin al-Hasan al-Askari, the 12th Imam, the Expected One. He was born in Samarrah, Iraq, to a slave girl name Narjis. He has not interacted with his followers since 940 A.D.; he is said to have been "occulted" since then. He is believed, by some, to be alive somewhere in Saudi Arabia today.

The Vision of Fatima

On May 13, 1917, three children apparently saw a vision of a lady who identified herself as the Lady of the Rosary. This occurred at Fatima, Santerem district, in central Portugal. The vision was repeated on each subsequent month for a total of six visions, until October when a crowd of 70,000 apparently witnessed some kind of solar phenomena.

On May 13, 1981, Pope John Paul believes he was saved from an assassination attempt while stooping to examine a young girl's pendant commemorating the Vision of Fatima. He is now heavily influenced by messages associated with it and with the end-times.[19]

Who was Fatima? Fatima (*Az-Sahra*, "the Shining One") was the daughter of Muhammad. (Other sons and daughters died or failed to reproduce.)

To the Shi'ites, Fatima is very important since she married Ali, whom the Shi'ites consider to be the only legitimate heir to the authority of the Prophet Muhammad and gave them the 1st of their Imams through her son Husayn.[20]

The majority of the Muslims are of the Sunni sect of Islam. The Shi'ites, while fewer in number tend to be more militant, and follow after the direct descent from Ali and Fatima.[21]

The Peace Negotiations

It is of paramount importance to realize that the entire "Peace Process" presently dominating the policies of the West *is based on a false premise*.

It is not the *size* of Israel that is the problem: it is the *existence* of Israel that is the problem. All of Islam is irrevocably committed to the total destruction of Israel.

And, thus, the perpetual frustration of the world will endure right up to the end. Zechariah declared that Jerusalem would be "a cup of trembling" and a "burdensome stone"[22] for all who would deal with it--right up to the climax which we can now see being positioned.

It is the Islamic obsession with Israel that will lead to the Ultimate Jihad in Ezekiel 38. Let's take a closer look at it.

Endnotes:

1. Genesis 12:1ff.

2. Biblical use of the term "sin," however, comes from an old English archery term for
    "missing the mark."

3. McClintock and Strong, 6:406.

4. Koran: Sura 4:3.

5. Wives: Khadija, Sawda, Aesah (8 or 9 years old), Omm Salama, Hafsa,
    Zaynab (originally Jahsh's, Muhammad's adopted son's wife), Jowayriya,
    Omm Habiba, Safiya, Maymuna (of Hareth), Fatema, Hend, Asma (of
    Saba), Zaynab (of Khozayma), Habla, Asma (of Noman).
    Others: Mary (the Coptic Christian; chose to remain a slave rather than
    convert), Rayhana, Omm Sharik, Maymuna, Zaynab (a 3rd one), Khawla.

6. Koran: Suras 55; 72; 113, 114.

7. Biblical injunctions: Deuteronomy 4:19; 17:3; Job 31:26-28.
    Penalties: Deuteronomy 17:6; 2 Kings 23:5.

8. Michael Nazar-Ali, *Islam: A Christian Perspective*, Westminster Press,
    Philadelphia, 1983, p. 21; Alfred Guillaume, *Islam*, Penguin Books, London, 1954,
    p. 6; Augustus H. Stong, *Systematic Theology*, Judson Press, Valley Forge PA,
    1976, p. 186.

9. Dr. M. Baravmann, *The Spiritual Background of Early Islam*, E. J. Brill, Leiden,
    1972; Dr. Jane Smith, *An Historical and Semitic Study of the Term Islam as Seen in
    a Sequence of Quran Commentaries*, University of Montana Press, for Harvard
    University Dissertations, 1970. Dr. Robert Morey, *The Islamic Invasion*.

10. Robert Morey, *The Islamic Invasion*, Harvest House, Eugene OR, p.48;
    Encyclopedia of Religion and Ethics, ed. James Hastings, T & T Clark, Edinburgh,
    1908, I:326; *Encyclopedia of Religion*, eds. Paul Meagher, Thomas O'Brien,
    Consuela Aherne, Corpus Pubilsihers, Washington DC, 1979, I:117; *Encyclopedia
    Britannica*, I:643; *Encyclopedia of Islam*, E.J. Brill, Leiden, 1913, I:302; I:406;
    III:1093.

11. Ali Dashti, *23 Years: A Study of the Prophetic Career of Mohammad*, George Allen
    & Unwin, London, 1985, pp. 48, 50.

12. J. A. Thompson, *The Bible and Archeology*, Wm. B. Eerdmans Pub. Co., Grand
    Rapids MI, 1965, pp.13-16.

13. For a detailed discussion, see Morey, p.158.

14. Isaiah 8:20.

15. Galatians 3:28.

16. Bat Ye'or, *The Dhimmi: Jews and Christians Under Islam*, Farleigh Dickinson University Press, 1965.

17. John 5:43.

18. 2 Thessalonians 2:4.

19. For an incisive study about this, and other Biblical aspects of Roman Catholicism, see *A Woman Rides the Beast*, by Dave Hunt,(Harvest House, Eugene OR 1994); it is a must read for anyone who takes the Bible seriously.

20. The famous martyr of Karbala. (Jassim M. Hussain, The Occultation of the Twelfth Imam, Muhammadi Trust, London, 1982. p. 17.)

21. A geneological tree is included in the briefing package, *The Sword of Allah,* which includes two tape cassettes and other notes and references.

22. Zechariah 12:2, 3ff.

Chapter 10:

The Invasion of Ezekiel 38

And thou shalt come from thy place out of the north parts, thou, and many people with thee, all of them riding upon horses, a great company, and a mighty army:

And thou shalt come up against my people of Israel, as a cloud to cover the land; it shall be in the latter days, and I will bring thee against my land, that the heathen may know me, when I shall be sanctified in thee, O Gog, before their eyes.

Ezekiel 38:15, 16

Let's review the Ezekiel passage in detail. Ezekiel 37 includes the famous Vision of the Dry Bones. This remarkable vision is interpreted within the passage itself and predicts the regathering of Israel back into their land.[1] This has been dramatically fulfilled in recent years.

In Ezekiel 40 through 48, the Scripture details the Millennial Temple to be built when the Lord establishes His Kingdom on the earth. There is a major, climactic, event that occurs after the regathering of Israel (Chapter 37) and the establishment of the kingdom (Chapters 40 onwards). That event is the ill-fated invasion detailed in Chapters 38 and 39.

The first six verses have been dealt with in the preceding chapters. Let us begin our review with verse 7:

> *Be thou prepared, and prepare for thyself,*
> *thou, and all thy company that are assembled unto*
> *thee, and be thou a guard unto them.*
>
> Ezekiel 38:7

The term *"guard"* depicts being both their leader and their provider. It is provocative that, indeed, Magog (Russia) is presently the provider of weapons and technology to the very allies listed. (The technologies involved are revealed in Ezekiel 39 and examined in the next chapter.)

After many days thou shalt be visited: in the latter years thou shalt come into the land that is brought back from the sword, and is gathered out of many people, against the mountains of Israel, which have been always waste: but it is brought forth out of the nations, and they shall dwell safely all of them.

Ezekiel 38:8

The precondition of this invasion is the regathering of Israel into the land. After almost two thousand years of being dispersed, we have witnessed the miracle of their regathering precisely as the Bible predicted.[2]

Thou shalt ascend and come like a storm, thou shalt be like a cloud to cover the land, thou, and all thy bands, and many people with thee.

Ezekiel 38:9

It is also noteworthy that the allies are all Islamic countries and, thus, are united in their hatred of Israel, their denial of Israel's right to exist, and their mutual commitment to undertake Israel's destruction.

Thus saith the Lord GOD; It shall also come to pass, that at the same time shall things come into thy mind, and thou shalt think an evil thought:

And thou shalt say, I will go up to the land of unwalled villages; I will go to them that are at rest, that dwell safely, all of them dwelling without walls, and having neither bars nor gates...

Ezekiel 38:10, 11

The dwelling "safely" employs the word, *betach,* which can mean *in false confidence;* not necessarily in *physical* security, as the English translation would imply.[3]

The reference to "unwalled villages" is interesting. Ezekiel himself probably had never seen an *unwalled* village. Jerusalem today is not a walled city. For most of the troubled centuries, the dwellers inside the ancient walled city suffered miserable living conditions. Yet, outside the walls robbers and brigands roamed the area and no one wanted to be caught outside the walls at night.

However, the prophet Zechariah wrote some 2,500 years earlier:

> *And said unto him, Run, speak to this young man, saying, Jerusalem shall be inhabited as towns without walls for the multitude of men and cattle therein.*
>
> *Zechariah 2:4*

When a British Jew, Sir Moses Montefiore, began building houses outside the walls of Jerusalem in the mid-1800's, no one would live in them until he hired a private security police force to protect the people. (Montefiore's windmill still stands in Jerusalem today.) Today, of course, there are, indeed, no walls as protection for the inhabitants.

An Attractive Target

> *To take a spoil, and to take a prey; to turn thine hand upon the desolate places that are now*

> *inhabited, and upon the people that are gathered*
> *out of the nations, which have gotten cattle and*
> *goods, that dwell in the midst of the land.*
>
> Ezekiel 38:12

It is interesting that the preconditions for the invasion have been met today. Israel has been regathered from all nations into their own land and has turned that land which was a desert wasteland for 1,900 years, into the fruit basket of Europe. A country which is ⅓ the size of San Bernardino County in California has now become the fourth largest exporter of fruit in the world.

The stage is set.

The Gainsayers

> *Sheba, and Dedan, and the merchants of*
> *Tarshish, with all the young lions thereof, shall say*
> *unto thee, Art thou come to take a spoil? hast thou*
> *gathered thy company to take a prey? to carry away*
> *silver and gold, to take away cattle and goods, to*
> *take a great spoil?*
>
> Ezekiel 38:13

Sheba and Dedan were cities in what is now Saudi Arabia. It is interesting that they are *not* directly involved in the invasion: they are on the sidelines as critics, apparently with lip service only. (In chapter 13 we will see why Saudi Arabia is nervously on the sidelines!)

Tarshish

Tarshish is a tough one to identify. We know that it was associated with ships and extensive shipping trade, and apparently was an island. It was well-known throughout the ancient world.

Tarshish first appears as one of the sons of Javan, a brother of Magog, both sons of Japheth.[4] Numerous Scriptural references clearly identify a country named Tarshish as a very remote sea-trading island, as much as three years distant.[5] Jonah, in fleeing his call to Nineveh and attempting to escape as far away as possible, boarded a ship to Tarshish.[6]

Some have identified Tarshish with Ceylon, some with the East Indies, and some with Sardinia and Tarteusess in southern Spain.

Others have suggested Britain. Tarshish was known as a source of tin. "Britannia" means a source of tin. Archaeological discoveries incident to the Stonehenge monument on the Salisbury Plain in Britain also indicate that the Wessex people enjoyed trade with the Eastern Mediterranean as early as 1500 B.C.[7]

This leads to conjectures as to whom the "Young Lions" refers. From the possible identification of Tarshish with Britain, some find the suggestion of its colonies (the United States) irresistible. But this all does seem a bit tenuous.

The Lost Ten Tribes

These views also are usually accompanied by variations on the conjecture that the "Lost Ten Tribes" of Israel ultimately wandered off through Europe and are somehow linked to various royal families. These are colorful legends, but arise due to a misreading of the Biblical text.

Accompanying some of the legends of the so-called "Ten Lost Tribes" are aspersions on the present State of Israel and the people being regathered in the Land. These various theories such as "British Israelism" are by their nature anti-Semitic because they deny the Jewish people their proper place in the plan of God.

Before the Assyrian captivity, substantial numbers from the northern tribes had identified themselves with the House of David.[8] The rebellion of Jeroboam, and subsequent crises, caused many to repudiate the northern kingdom and unite with the southern kingdom in a common alliance to the House of David and to worship the Lord.[9] Likewise, those favoring idol worship, established under Jeroboam, migrated north.

When the northern kingdom went into captivity (722 B.C.), all twelve tribes were represented in the south. God even addressed the 12 tribes in the south.[10] When the Babylonians took the southern kingdom into captivity (586 B.C.), members of all 12 tribes of Israel were involved. Isaiah, prophesying to Judah, referred to them as the "House of Jacob, which are called by the name of Israel . . . "[11]

After the Babylonian captivity, the terms Jew and Israelite are used interchangeably.[12]   The remnant who returned from Babylon is represented as the nation.[13]

In the New Testament, our Lord is said to have offered Himself to the nation, "the lost sheep of the house of Israel."[14] The tribes are frequently referred to in other New Testament passages.[15]

In Ezekiel 37, the Dry Bones Vision, declares that Judah (the Jews) and Israel (the ten tribes) shall be joined as one in the regathering.[16] This is true today. Israel is being regathered just as God has announced.

Whose People?

Therefore, son of man, prophesy and say unto Gog, Thus saith the Lord GOD; In that day when my people of Israel dwelleth safely, shalt thou not know it?

Ezekiel 38:14

Note the reference to "my people." That's an interesting possessive used by God Himself. The naive Bible reader usually will assume that God always refers to Israel as "His people." However, when one studies God's dealings with Israel carefully, one will discover that there was predicted a time when they were to be set aside as "not my people."[17] After an interval, God will again take them up as His special people.[18] During the interval, God deals expressly through the Church. (Some of the implications of this will be explored in chapter 16.)

The Forces Appear

> *And thou shalt come from thy place out of*
> *the north parts, thou, and many people with thee,*
> *all of them riding upon horses, a great company,*
> *and a mighty army...*
>
> Ezekiel 38:15

The "north parts" is literally the "extreme, or uttermost" parts of the north. Even without other background, any globe reveals Magog's identity, as the people from the uttermost part of the north from Israel: obviously, the Russians.

Don't be confused by the references to "horses." The Hebrew word is סוס, *soos*, which means "leaper." While it is usually translated "horse" it can also mean bird,[19] or even chariot-rider.[20]

(My wife and one of my daughters are horse lovers. Personally, I prefer mine 200 at a time, under a hood.)

This description is simply 2,500-year-old language which describes a mechanized force. We still call motorized infantry "cavalry" even today. Israel's main battle tank is the *Merkeva*, or "Chariot."

Whose Land?

> *And thou shalt come up against my people of*
> *Israel, as a cloud to cover the land; it shall be in*
> *the latter days, and I will bring thee against my*
> *land, that the heathen may know me, when I shall*
> *be sanctified in thee, O Gog, before their eyes.*

Ezekiel 38:16

Again, the possessive "my land" is significant. This land doesn't belong to Israel, or to the Palestinians, but to God Himself. The Bible portrays the entire world going to arms over the land of Israel and we see it being positioned already.

(The ultimate land grant to Israel goes all the way to the River Euphrates.[21] Whenever someone speaks of the "West Bank," I am tempted to ask, "Of which river?")

Also, the term "latter days" clearly identifies this as end time prophecy, just prior to the "Day of the Lord."

God's Purpose

> *Thus saith the Lord GOD; Art thou he of whom I have spoken in old time by my servants the prophets of Israel, which prophesied in those days many years that I would bring thee against them?*

Ezekiel 38:17

God always declares His actions in advance through His prophets.[22]

> *And it shall come to pass at the same time when Gog shall come against the land of Israel,*
>
> *saith the Lord GOD, that my fury shall come up in my face.*

Ezekiel 38:18

This is not because Israel *deserves* His help: it is because *His reputation* is on the line. God has announced to the nations that He would do this, in His own words, for "His Name's sake." He has declared to the heathen nations that He will do this; His righteousness is, in effect, at stake!

> *And I scattered them among the heathen, and they were dispersed through the countries: according to their way and according to their doings I judged them.*
>
> *And when they entered unto the heathen, whither they went, they profaned my holy name, when they said to them, These are the people of the Lord, and are gone forth out of his land.*
>
> *But I had pity for mine holy name, which the house of Israel had profaned among the heathen, whither they went.*
>
> *Therefore say unto the house of Israel, Thus saith the Lord God; I do not this for your sakes, O house of Israel, but for mine holy name's sake, which ye have profaned among the heathen, whither ye went.*
>
> *And I will sanctify my great name, which was profaned among the heathen, which ye have profaned in the midst of them; and the heathen shall know that I am the Lord, saith the Lord God, when I shall be sanctified in you before their eyes.*
>
> *For I will take you from among the heathen, and gather you out of all countries, and will bring you into your own land.*
>
> Ezekiel 36:19-24

God's Methods

> *For in my jealousy and in the fire of my wrath have I spoken, Surely in that day there shall be a great shaking in the land of Israel;*
>
> *So that the fishes of the sea, and the fowls of the heaven, and the beasts of the field, and all creeping things that creep upon the earth, and all the men that are upon the face of the earth, shall shake at my presence, and the mountains shall be thrown down, and the steep places shall fall, and every wall shall fall to the ground.*
>
> Ezekiel 38:19, 20

This event will include an earthquake that is felt around the world! I don't know what it will be on the Richter scale, but it should be a record.

> *And I will call for a sword against him throughout all my mountains, saith the Lord GOD: every man's sword shall be against his brother.*
>
> *And I will plead against him with pestilence and with blood; and I will rain upon him, and upon his bands, and upon the many people that are with him, an overflowing rain, and great hail-stones, fire, and brimstone.*
>
> *Ezekiel 38:21, 22*

This begins to sound like nuclear warfare, doesn't it? We will discuss the weapons technology in the next chapter which explores the text of Ezekiel 39.

Endnotes:

1. Ezekiel 37:11ff.

2. Isaiah 11:11, et al.

3. *Betach* appears 162 times in the Old Testament; 130 times it means in false confidence, as a state of mind, in contrast to *physical* security.

4. Genesis 10:2, 4; 1 Chronicles 1:7.

5. 1 Kings 10:22; 22:48. 2 Chronicles 9:21; 20:36,37; Estther 1:14; Psalm 48:7; 72:10; Isaiah 2:16; 23:1,6,10,14; 60:9; 66:19; Jeremiah 10:9; Ezekiel 27:12, 25.

6. John 1:3; 4:2.

7. Gerald Hawkins, *Stonehenge Decoded*,

8. 1 Kings 12:16-20; 2 Chronicles 11:16-17.

9. 2 Chronicles 15:9; 19:4; 30:1, 10-11, 25-26; 34:5-7, 22; 30:5, 6, 10-11, 21; 34:9; 35:17-18; etc.

10. 2 Chronicles 11:3.

11. Isaiah 48:1. Cf. vv12-14.

12. Ezra calls the returning remnant Jews 8 times and Israel 40 times. Ezra speaks of "all Israel": Ezra 2:70; 3:11; 8:35; 10:25, et al. Nehemiah calls them Jews 11 times, Israel 22 times. Nehemiah speaks of "all Israel" being back in the land: Nehemiah 12:47.

13. Malachi 1:1.

14. Matthew 10:5-6; 15:24.

15. Matthew 4:13,15; Luke 2:36; Acts 4:36; Philippians 3:5; "the twelve tribes" Acts 26:7; James 1:1. Anna knew her tribal identity from the tribe of Asher (Luke 2:30). Paul knew he was of the tribe of Benjamin (a "Jew" and an "Israelite") Romans 11:1. The New Testament speaks of Israel 75 times and uses the word "Jew" 174 times. (Acts 21:39; 22:3; Romans 11:1; 2 Cor 11:22; Phil 3:5, etc.)

16. Ezekiel 37:16-17, 21-22.

17. Hosea 1:9,10.

18. Hosea 2:23; Romans 11:25.

19. Jeremiah 8:7.

20. Exodus 14:9.

21. Land Grant: Genesis 15:7-8, 13-16; 17:8; Deuteronomy 28-30; Jeremiah 30-31; Ezekiel 36.
Boundaries: Genesis 15:18-21; Exodus 23:24-31; Numbers 34:1-14; Joshua 1:3; Ezekiel 47:13ff. From the "River of Egypt" to the Euphrates: from eastern Egypt, past Damascus, all the way into western Iraq.

22. Amos 3:7; Habakkuk 1:5.

Section IV

Strategic Update

*"Somewhere, sometime--but in this decade--somebody...
is going to set off a nuclear weapon in deadly earnest."*

Rear Adm. Edward D. Schafer Jr.
Director of Naval Intelligence

Chapter 11:

The Technology of Ezekiel 39

And I will plead against him with pestilence and with blood; and I will rain upon him, and upon his bands, and upon the many people that are with him, an overflowing rain, and great hailstones, fire, and brimstone.

Ezekiel 38:22

And I will send a fire on Magog, and among them that dwell securely in the isles: and they shall know that I am the LORD.

Ezekiel 39:6

Before we delve further into our exploration of the results of this Ultimate Jihad, let's examine the strategic environment that you and I are presently faced with.

Nuclear Proliferation

We have enjoyed a period of nuclear stability that has lasted five decades. This stability has been the result of a doctrine known as "Mutually Assured Destruction." While not very popular in the press, and certainly not free of occasional tensions, it worked. It was based on three presuppositions:

1)   Only two adversaries were involved: the USSR and the USA;

2)   there existed a nominal balance of power between the opponents; and

3)   both opponents were rational.

All three of these essential presuppositions are totally obsolete today.

1)   *There are no longer only two adversaries* in possession of nuclear weapons. The nightmare that plagued the

strategic think tanks of the 1950's and 60's was known as the "Nth Country Problem."[1] We all dreaded the inevitable day when rogue elements would be able to blackmail--or worse--the major nations into submitting to their demands.

There are now more than 11 Third World countries in the nuclear community, and the candidate protagonists are growing.[2] More than 22 countries are presently developing intercontinental ballistic missiles.[3] 66 countries presently have the capability to launch surface-skimming cruise missiles. And these numbers increase daily.[4]

2)   *There is no longer a stable balance of power:* there is a race of desperation going on. The first Muslim that can lob a nuclear device into the nation of Israel will be a hero without peer throughout the entire Islamic community.

3)   The opponents presently acquiring these capabilities *are not,* what we could consider in the Western world, *rational.* How do you survive a "chicken race" with someone who believes he goes to heaven if he loses?

During a private briefing at NATO Headquarters in Brussels, Robert Hunter, our Ambassador to NATO, declared that, "A nuclear confrontation in the Middle East is not just likely, it is certain. It is just a matter of timing."

Robin Beard, Assistant Secretary of Defense, at that same meeting, admitted to me, "When the Soviets were in power, we knew the procedures in place to prevent an accident. Today, we don't even know who has the button--and there's a power grab going on."

Jesus described a time when *"there would be no flesh saved except those days be shortened."*[5]

Until now, the technology wasn't available to treat that prediction literally. How could this have been true in the 17th or 18th centuries? The ominous cloud of this very capability now hangs over every political and military decision made on the Planet Earth.

Biblical Battles

As a graduate of the U.S. Naval Academy--and as student of the Bible for more than 50 years--you can appreciate that I have had a special interest in the various battles of the Scriptures. As one studies the many military confrontations in the Bible--both historical and those predicted--the structure of the text is usually the same: two parties engage; there is a conclusion; and the narrative moves on. When Israel was acting in response to God's direction, she often won against staggering odds. When Israel was "out of fellowship,"she got clobbered.

But in no case is there any language devoted to the "clean up" after the battle. Here in Ezekiel 39, there is virtually *an entire chapter* devoted to the clean up of the battlefield. Why?

Since we have in our hands, indeed, an integrated message--consisting of 66 books, penned by 40 authors over thousands of years--and since this is manifestly of supernatural design and intent, we would expect that there is nothing trivial nor accidental in the text. It would appear that the details of this clean up are there to indicate the *technologies employed!*

Vocabulary

We should not let the classic vocabulary deter us from the real intended message of the writer. We have already noted that the use of "horses" (*soos*, or "leaper")[6] may simply be idiomatic of motorized infantry. There are other possible examples:

> *And I will smite thy bow out of thy left hand, and will cause thine arrows to fall out of thy right hand.*
>
> Ezekiel 39:3

These "bows and arrows" may be more in the minds of the translators, speaking of 1611 A.D. technology. These terms could be regarded as synechdoches (terms where the specific is used to imply the general; or the general for the specific, etc.), such as חֶרֶב (*keh-rev*), as for a destroying instrument, or "sword." This term is used today to suggest any form of arms.

Other examples could be חֵצִי (*khayts*), for a piercing missile: "arrow"; or קֶשֶׁת (*keh-sheth*), for its associated launcher: a "bow." These terms could easily be idiomatic for "launchers" and "missiles."

The Technology Revealed

> *And they that dwell in the cities of Israel shall go forth, and shall set on fire and burn the weapons, both the shields and the bucklers, the bows and the arrows, and the handstaves, and the spears, and they shall burn them with fire seven years:*

So that they shall take no wood out of the field, neither cut down any out of the forests; for they shall burn the weapons with fire: and they shall spoil those that spoiled them, and rob those that robbed them, saith the Lord GOD.

Ezekiel 39:9, 10

The weapons left over from the battle provide all of the energy needs of Israel for seven years. This doesn't sound like conventional weapons, does it? Ezekiel seems to have anticipated our nuclear age 2,500 years ago.

Development contracts have recently been granted to develop the technology to convert warheads into electricity.[7] But why "seven years?"

Nuclear Shelf Life

It may come as a surprise to many to learn that a nuclear warhead *has a limited shelf life.*

If you are Rafsanjani of Iran, Assad of Syria, or "Daffy" Khadafi of Libya, and you acquire a nuclear warhead (without having reprocessing facilities), you have a problem: You either *use* it or *lose* it!

The life of nuclear material depends upon many factors, including the type and quality. A nuclear warhead depends on a very delicate geometric balance.

At the center of a nuclear warhead is a sphere, about the size of an overgrown grapefruit, of either uranium-235 or plutonium-239. (U-235 occurs in nature as an isotope of uranium and must be separated from the U-238 more common material.) Pu-239 is made artificially in "breeder" reactors.[8]

A subcritical mass of fissionable material is at the center of a sphere of shaped explosive charges. The detonation of the explosives compresses the fissionable material to a supercritical mass, which, when neutrons are released, causes a chain reaction yielding enormous thermal and radioactive energy.[9]

Implosion Device

Fissionable Core

Shaped Explosive Charges

Tamper/Reflector

Tritium Gas

In a thermonuclear (hydrogen) warhead, the fissionable material is surrounded with "heavy" hydrogen (tritium) which, when initiated by the nuclear fission, becomes the even more powerful chain reaction of fusion--an increase in yield of megatons.

[When I served in the Air Force, we had one megaton warheads. Today, the Russians have (a few) 100 megaton warheads in inventory. A few of these, detonated at the same time, could alter the orbit of the earth.]

Impurities in the fissionable material--such as short-lived isotopes--can subtlely alter the critical geometry of the material to render it unreliable. The breeder reactors used in producing the plutonium for the Russian warheads generate material with impurities that yield a predicted shelf-life of only seven years. They must be reprocessed on a six-year turnover cycle.[10]

(With much fanfare, we read in the press that Ukraine has returned their nuclear warheads to Russia, after receiving $1 billion in U.S. aid.[11] What they didn't tell you is that they had *expired*.)

I wonder if there is a relationship between this technology background and the Biblical text? If so, how did Ezekiel know that?

But there's more.

Disposal Procedures

And it shall come to pass in that day, that I
will give unto Gog a place there of graves in Israel,

the valley of the passengers on the east of the sea:
and it shall stop the noses of the passengers: and
there shall they bury Gog and all his multitude:
and they shall call it The valley of Hamon-gog.
Ezekiel 39:11

They pick a place east of the Dead Sea: downwind.

And they shall sever out men of continual
employment, passing through the land to bury with
the passengers those that remain upon the face of
the earth, to cleanse it: after the end of seven
months shall they search.
Ezekiel 39:14

They apparently wait seven months before they enter the battlefield. Why?

They "sever out men of continual employment," which is quaint old English for the *hire of professionals*. Why?

And seven months shall the house of Israel
be burying of them, that they may cleanse the land.
Ezekiel 39:12

Sounds like a major mess. But Ezekiel doesn't stop there:

And the passengers that pass through the
land, when any seeth a man's bone, then shall he
set up a sign by it, till the buriers have buried it in
the valley of Hamongog.

If any of the "passengers"--travelers, or tourists--that happen to find a bone which the professionals have missed--*he*

doesn't touch it! He sets up a sign by it and lets the professionals deal with it.

Any of our readers who have been trained or briefed on
Nuclear, Biological and Chemical Warfare ("NBC" procedures)
will certainly recognize these instructions.[12]

(Other technologies also seem to be alluded to in the
Scriptures. In Zechariah we find what appears to be a description of the effects of a neutron bomb[13]--a device Israel has
developed, but the U.S. has not. Also, it is interesting that
worldwide television is implied in the Olivet Discourse.[14])

A Nuclear *Exchange*?

> *And I will send a fire on Magog, and among*
> *them that dwell securely in the isles: and they shall*
> *know that I am the LORD.*
>
> Ezekiel 39:6

For many, this is one of the most troubling verses of all.
Who are "them that dwell securely in the isles?"

The term for "isles" (Hebrew, אִיִּים; Greek,LXX, νῆσοι),
can mean coastlands, or continents. It seems to derive from a
root suggesting a remote, pleasant place. Those who "dwell
securely in the isles" could be a veiled hint of the United States.

Some analysts see an intercontinental nuclear exchange
possibly suggested. With the proliferation of nuclear weapons
throughout the world today, such a prospect is disturbingly
likely.[15] The possibility of some "eleventh hour" sabre-rattling
escalating into a real exchange is only too easily to visualize.

Brinkmanship

It almost happened once before, during the Cuban Missile Crisis. In 1961, our satellite reconnaissance had revealed the installation of missiles in Cuba. Russian ships were continuing to supply Cuba in defiance of the U.S. protestations. The media focused on the naval embargo which had been ordered. However, there was a more serious drama going on.

I was with John Rubin, Assistant Secretary of Defense, at the time. President John F. Kennedy had ordered all of our strategic assets--the Strategic Air Command and all of the Atlas and Titan resources--put on alert, and, in the well-publicized speech, being hand-delivered to the Kremlin, he warned that if even one missile is fired anywhere in the Western Hemisphere *it would result in a full scale retaliation against the Soviet Union.*

It was an intense time. We all watched apprehensively until, finally, the Russian ships turned around and the crisis de-escalated to everyone's relief.

(What would have happened if some Cuban technician inadvertently fired some tactical device into Central America, or wherever? The unthinkable consequences were frightening.)

This could happen again. As Israel comes under attack, the U.S., once again, might attempt a show of brinksmanship, but this time it all goes awry. The U.S. missiles might provide the "hailstones of fire"--and vice versa.

Ezekiel 38 appears increasingly timely the more we understand the passage.

Summary

The description of the technology implied in this passage is one of the reasons it has become so well-known. Very impressive, for having been penned more than 2500 years ago.

In December 1942, physicists Enrico Fermi and Leo Szilard lingered in a squash court under the west stands of the University of Chicago stadium. They had just achieved the first self-sustaining fission reaction and knew the atomic bomb was now closer to reality. Szilard shook hands with Fermi and said, "This day will go down as a black day in the history of mankind."

The technology they helped unleash ended one great war, and for five decades the world remained in a tense balance without disaster. How about the next few decades?

Hal Lindsey has pointed out that the weapons which will be used at Armageddon are probably in inventory today. The remaining chapters in this section will summarize the intelligence horizon presently facing us.

End notes:

1. One of my early contributions was to design the original computer-assisted war gaming simulations supporting the Arms Control Negotiations in Geneva in the early 1960's.

2. Four of them, Israel, India, Pakistan and South Africa, already possess a nuclear capability; North Korea, Argentina, Brazil, Taiwan, and Iran are said to be right behind them, with Libya and Iraq expected to become nuclear within a few years.

3. These are listed in chapter 13.

4. See *Strategic Trends of the 1990's*, Koinonia House. Also, we publish a monthly intelligence news journal highlighting the Biblical relevance of current events. There should be an introductory gift certificate included in this book, or call 1-(800)-KHOUSE1 or write P.O. Box D, Coeur d'Alene ID 83816.

5. Mattew 24:22; Mark 13:20.

6. Jeremiah 8:7, "bird"; Exodus 14:9, chariot rider.

7. General Atomics of San Diego (*New York Times*, 25 January 1994); Combustion Engineering Inc, of Brown Boveri Inc. (Business Week, May 16, 1994). Sandia Nationa Laboratories and Alliant Techsystems are even exploring the conversion of explosives and rocket propellants into synthetic fuel gas for industrial turbines.

8. Subsequent reactions can cause the Pu-239 to capture more neutrons, forming Pu-240 and Pu-241, which are highly radioactive and tend to undergo nuclear fission spontaneously.

9. For an excellent summary of how Iraq reverse engineered the technology, see *IEEE Spectrum*, April 1992.

10. Norman Friedman, "The Russian Meltdown Continues," *U. S. Naval Institute Proceedings,* April 1992, p. 124.

11. *Reuters*, July 17, 1995.

12. Cf. *Opeator's Manual for Marking Set, Contamination: Nuclear, Biological, Chemical (NBC) (9905-12-124-5955),* Technical Manual 3-9905-001-10, Headquarters, Department of the Army.

13. Zechariah 14:12.

14. Matthew 24:15 describes an event within the Holy of Holies, "seen" by those who are throughout Judea. On CNN?

15. There are, at present, in the "Third World" alone, 22 nations developing and manufacturing ballistic missiles. 11 of them have nuclear capability.

Chapter 12:

Russia Today

All warfare is based on deception. When you are are strong, appear weak. When you are weak appear strong.

SunTzu, 5th century B.C.

"Comrades, do not be concerned about all you hear about glasnost and perestroika and democracy in the coming years. These are primarily for outward consumption. There will be no significant internal change within the Soviet Union other than for cosmetic purposes. Our purpose is to disarm the Americans and let them fall asleep . . . "

Soviet President Mikhail Gorbachev,
Soviet Politburo, November 1987:

T he enigma of Russia today challenges the most informed experts, and the more that one knows, the more enigmatic it becomes.

Their Strategic Dilemma

Their economy appears in shambles, and yet their military is the most formidable the world has ever seen. Russia is desperately dependent upon the export of arms and raw materials. Defense Minister Pavel Grachev expects the increase in 1995 to exceed 40% over last year. And their defense industries are still only at 10-15% capacity.

Their strategic horizon--both east and west--is dominated by traditional enemies. As they look west, they see a German dominated European Union--traditional enemies with their own exclusive agenda.

As they look east, they see China and Japan beginning to pool their resources--again, both being traditional enemies. Combining the capital and technology of Japan with the labor and raw materials of China is expected to spark the biggest economic boom the Planet Earth has ever seen.

While Russia has been exporting technology and advance armaments to China, Moscow is waking up to the reality that they are creating their own worst nightmare. They are facilitating a country with an economy that will soon exceed that of the United States--with more than four times the population--across a land border that is totally indefensible. The tide of the population growth of China--*5 million excess each year*--is one of Beijing's most effective strategic "weapons."

Russia has no alternative but to develop a new power base to the south. As the analysts have been predicting, they are embracing the radical Muslim nations.

They have already signed military assistance treaties with Iran, the republics of Central Asia, and perhaps others. They can hardly avoid being entangled in the Islamic agenda for the destruction of Israel.

> *Thus saith the Lord God; Behold, I am against thee, O Gog, the chief prince of Meshech and Tubal:*
> *And I will turn thee back, and put hooks into thy jaws, and I will bring thee forth, and all thine army.*
>
> *Ezekiel 38:3, 4*

The "hooks in the jaws" (a severe reining device like a hackamore) seem to indicate that Magog will be drawn forcibly into the ill-fated invasion the Bible has been predicting.

Strategic Doctrines

If we desire to understand the posture of Russia, we also need to understand their long term strategic doctrines.

The transactional model of the United States is poker: each "hand" is a negotiation which is, to a large extent, *history independent*. As Kenny Rogers has taught us, "You got to know when to hold 'em; and know when to fold 'em. 'Know when to walk away; and know when to run."

Unfortunately, there's no place to hide.

The negotiating model of Russia is more like chess. The entire game hangs on the *gambit*: knowing when to sacrifice something to gain a longer term--and, hopefully, decisive--advantage. The development of history is everything.

In the 1930's, Dimitri Manuilski, a political instructor at the Lenin School for Political Warfare (and the mentor of Mikhail Gorbachev) taught the necessity of deceiving the West prior to launching an all-out military assault.[1]

"War to the hilt between communism and capitalism is inevitable. Today, of course, we are not strong enough to attack. Our time will come in thirty to forty years. To win, we shall need the element of surprise. The bourgeoisie . . . will have to be put to sleep.

"So we shall begin by launching the most spectacular peace movement on record. There will be electrifying overtures and unheard of concessions. The capitalist countries, stupid and decadent, will rejoice to cooperate in their own destruction. They will leap at another chance to be friends.

"As soon as their guard is down, we will smash them with our clenched fist."

Since 1917, the communists have launched six separate "Glasnosts" to deceive the West and receive aid. Each time, Western leaders have rushed in to "save Russia."

In November 1987, Soviet President Mikhail Gorbachev made a speech to the Soviet Politburo:

"Comrades, do not be concerned about all you hear about glasnost and perestroika and democracy in the coming years. These are primarily for outward consumption. There will be no significant internal change within the Soviet Union other than for cosmetic purposes. Our purpose is to disarm the Americans and let them fall asleep. We want to accomplish three things:

> *One, we want the Americans to withdraw conventional forces from Europe.*

> *Two, we want them to withdraw nuclear forces from Europe.*

> *Three, we want the Americans to stop proceeding with the Strategic Defense Initiative."*

What's the scorecard? We have withdrawn several hundred thousand of our troops from Europe, leaving only a token force. President Bush ordered the withdrawal of all nuclear missiles from Europe, all nuclear weapons from American Navy ships, and eliminated the bomber alerts that have protected us for 50 years.

The Strategic Defense Initiative--exploiting technology to place weapons at risk rather than our cities at risk--was canceled. The astonishing onslaught on logic by an unprecedented media blitz effectively eliminated our only defense.

In 1991, in the wake of Desert Storm, Congress authorized the development of a national missile defense. However, the current administration scrapped the program on the grounds that there was no realistic missile threat to the United States.

With 23 countries presently building intercontinental ballistic missiles, it is difficult to understand the logic.[2]

(The famed "coup" of Gorbachev will be discussed in chapter 15.)

I once had the privilege of serving on a board of directors with Dr. Edward Teller, Chief Scientific Advisor to the President; General David C. Jones, Chairman of the Joint Chiefs of Staff; and Admiral Tom Hayward, Chief of Naval Operations. These three were, at the time, undoubtedly the best informed Americans on the Planet Earth regarding our strategic predicament.

As I had the opportunity to get to know them personally, I was startled to learn that, despite their very diversified personalities and backgrounds, they each lived their lives in a day-to-day fear of a preemptive nuclear strike by the Soviet Union!

We discussed the various reasons for this disturbing outlook. One of the most telling disclosures was that all of the training materials used to indoctrinate Russia's senior officers were designed on the assumption that, in any confrontation with the United States, *they* would have the advantage of surprise.

Their entire strategic doctrine, by which they trained their most senior leaders, was based on a preemptive first strike by them.

Yeltsin, in a 23-page document which was approved last year, reversed the previously announced Soviet policy denying a first strike doctrine (which no one took seriously), and openly declared that Russia is now ready *to launch nuclear missiles in a first strike*, if Russia, or its allies, are ever attacked with conventional weapons.

Strategic Resources

The Middle East provides the essential fuel for the Western industrial economy. Japan and Europe have less than 100 days of oil reserves. Even though Russia is the world's largest oil producer, inefficiencies and their own growing requirements have reduced the amount available for export. Middle Eastern oil dominates the foreign policies of Europe, and the hidden agendas of the U.S.

Their strategy toward the south is compelling. And what better prize to offer Islam than to deliver to them the land of Israel.

Russia, using our financial aid, is continuing to build and modernize their mammoth military establishment.

Russian Military

Russia's military establishment includes 4.8 million troops (including 350,000 secret police, interior ministry troops, and

Spetznaz special forces commandos.)[3]   Their morale is extremely low, and this is, of course, not a stabilizing factor.

This enormous force compares to less than two million American troops (of which only 500,000 are combat-ready soldiers.) Our current administration is, of course, dismantling America's armed forces as rapidly as possible. Jack Kemp notes that the U.S. is "cutting 15,000 personnel, one ship, 37 primary aircraft and one combat battalion each month." It is interesting that the closing of our bases is being monitored by Mikhail Gorbachev in his current role from his office in the Presidio in San Francisco. Who would ever have predicted this?[4]

The Russians have more than five times as many tanks and armored vehicles than America. In the event of war, the Russians can field more than 70,000 battle tanks, compared to 22,000 American tanks.[5] They are continuing to build 3,500 new tanks each year. We have stopped production of our M-1 tanks.

Missiles

Production of the SS-25, the most effective strategic missile due to its rapid mobility by truck or rail, is continuing. A completely new SS-25, with new technology, new composite materials, and greater accuracy, continues under development. The Russians are also now flight testing the new SS-N-20, their primary submarine-launched ballistic missile.

The capability to destroy any of our cities is still less than 30 minutes away.

The other Russian missile capabilities, as evidenced by the international arms markets, are also impressive. Their air-to-air R-77 is now viewed as superior to the AMRAAM; and the R-73 short-range air-to-air missile, with its 20 control surfaces and control devises, has no western counterpart. Its vectored thrust permits attacking in all directions--even rearward, a unique and decisive advantage in air combat.

The smart weapons that starred so conspicuously in the Gulf war, are also well represented in the Russian inventory. The Kh-58Yu is a supersonic anti-radar missile, bigger and faster than the U.S. HARM. It has a range of 125 miles: fired from Sarajevo, it could knock out an AWACS over the Adriatic.

The 8M30 Moskit anti-ship missile (SS-N-22), with its unique ramjet, cruises at Mach 2.5 (1,900 mph) at only tens of feet off the water. We understand the Ukraine has sold eight Moskits to Iran.[6]

The F-117 Stealth Fighter's principal weapon in the Gulf war was the GBU-27, a laser guided bomb with a penetrator warhead. The Russians' beTAB-500SchP has a rocket-boosted penetrator which has major advantages, and is apparently so accurate and lethal that its laser features are redundant.

Russian Navy

The Russian navy is substantially larger than the U. S. Navy. The Russians have 181 submarines, vs. 121 American submarines. (They are also developing a next generation while we are canceling ours.)

Typhoon Warnings

No review of Russian military power would be complete without a review of their strategic nuclear capability.

The nuclear-powered ballistic missile submarine is, in the view of many experts, the ultimate strategic weapon. Its unique combination of stealth and strategic nuclear delivery capabilities have rendered it far beyond simply the replacement of the capital ship or the means to destroy any surface fleet. These denizens can now circle the entire glove, each submarine holding at risk hundreds of cities, while itself is virtually invisible and immune to any effective counterattack. The nuclear submarine holds the advantage, not only over aircraft carriers, but any land-based (detectable and targetable) ballistic missile alternative.

The primary strategic deterrent of the United States is the Ohio Class Trident Submarine: 560 ft long, 42 ft. beam, 18,700 tons displacement, with 60,000 shaft horsepower from its nuclear reactor. It carries 24 missile tubes, each capable of carrying a Trident II D-5: a 5,000 mile range missile which puts hardened targets at risk.

The Russian equivalent is the ТАЙФУН, the Typhoon Class Ballistic Missile Submarine. It also is 561 ft long, but there the comparability ends. The Typhoon displaces 25,500 tons (with a 78 ft. beam vs. 42) and boasts *double titanium hulls.* (It is larger than the largest British cruiser in World War II). It has two power plants, two shafts, totaling 75,000 shaft horsepower. Unconfirmed reports indicate it can attain speeds in excess of 40 knots at 3,000 ft depths.

The Typhoon is armed with 20 missile tubes, each carrying 10 independently targeted warheads. Thus, *each Typhoon can hold 200 cities hostage.*

With 5,000 mile range missiles, it can operate from home waters. However, it is especially designed to operate under the ice of the Arctic. It has strengthened upper works, retractable hydroplanes, and other structural features designed to break through the ice, launch its weapons, and slip back into safety. Two closed-circuit TV cameras are positioned aft of the sail to observe the *polyas* as they break through.

But the key feature is that they are *silent.*

Antisubmarine Warfare Technology

The primary mission of the United States Navy is antisubmarine warfare. All of the Chiefs of Naval Operations, in recent years, have all been submarine veterans.[7]

Our entire antisubmarine warfare (ASW) technology has been built on the basis of facing a "noisy" adversary. In addition to onboard machine noise, propelling a craft through the water is normally accompanied by cavitation (bubble collapse), and other hydrodynamic phenomena. Our ASW assets rely, essentially, on passive sonar. The SOSUS Net, our sonobuoys, all are useful to the extent that the adversary emits sound that can be detected.

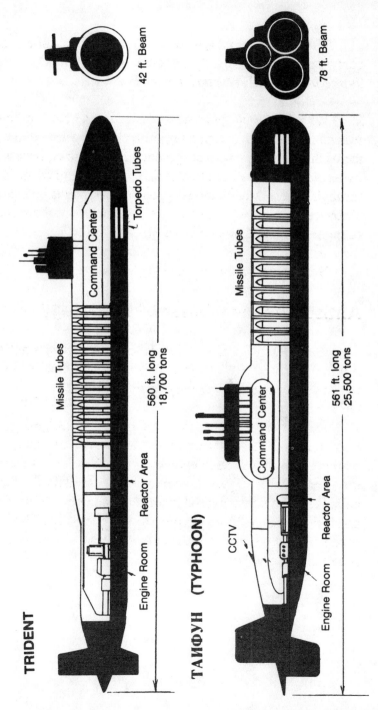

TRIDENT

42 ft. Beam

Torpedo Tubes

Command Center

Missile Tubes

Reactor Area

Engine Room

560 ft. long
18,700 tons

ТАЙФУН (TYPHOON)

78 ft. Beam

Missile Tubes

Command Center

CCTV

Reactor Area

Engine Room

561 ft. long
25,500 tons

The Typhoons, however, are now essentially silent. (That's one reason why Tom Clancy got in so much trouble, initially, with his famous novel, *The Hunt for Red October*. He hit a sensitive nerve.)

(The magnetohydrodynamic drive in his novel was not totally fanciful. This type of drive would appear to offer silent operation, avoiding cavitation and other sources of noise characteristic of conventional propulsion systems. Clancy's "caterpillar" form was fictional, but there does appear to be a strange VW-sized pod on the newer Akula Class Attack Submarines that some experts believe may be a magneto-hydrodyanmic drive.)

While the U.S. has had the advantage of facing a relatively noisy adversary, the Soviets did not. They faced a relatively quiet adversary. So they spent their research and development resources on "non-acoustic" technologies: magnetic and electrical fields, wake and thermal energy detection, bio-luminesence, etc. And they have made some significant breakthroughs.

There is reason to believe that they now have developed advanced laser techniques--using dual lasers from satellites or aircraft--which can now *track our Tridents in real time*.[8] They have an entire suite of reconaissance satellites continually monitoring our operations.[9] They now know where we are; which means that our strategic deterrent has been neutralized.

Yet we don't know where *they* are.

Advanced Development

Russia has also started developing a new advanced class of submarines called the *Severodvinsk*, expected to be operational by the year 2000. Improvements include quietness, sensor performance and weapons delivery, and are expected to outperform the U.S. best.

Current ASW techniques are also carrying the state of the art even further, with active sound cancellation, "white noise" masks, etc.

The Shkvall

The Russians have deployed an exceptionally high-speed underwater missile, code named the Shkval (Squall). It is reported to attain almost 200 knots, giving its target little opportunity to maneuver. It carries a tactical nuclear weapon and there are no known countermeasures, nor any counterpart in the west.

They appear to have solved the hydrodynamic problem with what they call *razrezhenyie* (vacuum, rarification, reduction, or thinness), probably by emitting gas bubbles--from an internal solid-fuel gas generator--within a double skin and then through perforations covering the entire missile body. It is assumed to be rocket-powered.

A higher speed (300 knots) guided version is also under development.

Economic Enigma

The provocative aspect of the Russian building program is the cost: a Trident (or a Typhoon) each cost in excess of $1 billion, fully equipped.

In 1988 we had 34 ballistic missile submarines commissioned; the Russians had 63. That gave them a capability to hold more than 12,000 cities hostage. Not bad. But, apparently, that isn't enough. Despite their desperate economic difficulties, they are still building more. Why?

Other weapons systems--bombers, tanks, etc.--have *multiple* missions. They can be used in a variety of assignments: defensive, offensive, interdiction, etc.

A ballistic missile submarine has but *one* use: a preemptive first strike.

It makes one ponder their strategic agenda that continues a commitment which alone might have saved the Soviet economy. What is their plan? And, who now controls the Typhoons? And where are they?

When I visited the NATO Headquarters, they admitted to me that they don't even know who has "the button."

The Secret Cities

Nuclear weapons and other strategic industries are located among the 87 secret cities, a vast network of research, design, production, testing, and storage sites spread across the breadth of the motherland. These do not appear on any maps--except those behind curtains in certain ministries. Tomsk-7, Arzamas-16, Chelyabinks-70, Krasnoyarsk-26, and others bear only postal numbers. Unlike our cities in the West, which are mixed industry economies, these are dedicated "single mission" government projects--completely integrated communities committed to their particular role or mission. (Similar to White Sands or Oak Ridge, but without being accompanied by other industries.)

My partner and I were the first Americans to be allowed into Selenograd--their "Silicon Valley"--located about 60 miles outside of Moscow. 60,000 population, and access is only with "special security arrangements."

As of January 1, 1995, the Ministry of Atomic Energy recorded 19 thefts of uranium from its enterprises.

Let's review how this southern strategy is affecting the Middle East.

Endnotes:

1. Assessing a leader's mentor can provide essential insights. Bill Clinton's admitted mentor is Carol Quigley, whose classic *Tragedy and Hope* is the blueprint for global one-world government.

2. The Middle East isn't the only powder keg: India, Pakistan, and China are significant nuclear powers, with tensions growing.

3. Defense Minister Pavel Grachev has alluded to only 2,431,000. Other sources, including the highly respected Institute for Soviet Studies, Frankfurt, Germany, has reported that Russia has twice as many men under arms as is officially acknowledged.

4. Anatoliy Golitsin did, in 1984, in his astonishing book, *New Lies For Old.*

5. The London-based International Institute for Strategic Studies estimates 25,000 tanks, 22,000 infantgry fighting vehicles, 23,000 armored personnel carriers, 22,500 artillery systems, 3,500 attack helicopters, and 800 operational-tactical missles. In addition, substantial stockpiles of tanks and artillery systems are held in storage east of the Urals.

6. The U.S. lacks the unique ramjet technology, and the Russians have declined to share it with the U.S., even now.

7. Admiral James Watkins (who became Secretary of Energy); Admiral Carlisle Trost (who was Brigade Commander when I was a plebe); and Admiral Frank Kelso (who was a classmate of mine--Class of '56).

8. A pulsed CO_2 laser creates an acostical pulse; a ultraviolet laser uses an interferometer technique known as "speckle backscatter." Using lithium niobate detector arrays, can locate a submarine at any depth within three pulses to within 50 ft. accuracy, within five minutes.

9. On Septermber 7, 1993, Russia launched Cosmos 2,262 in a 196 mile orbit, which not only transmits reconaissance images, it emits recoverable film posds. Current technology allows the determination of the make and model of cars in a parking lot from over 100 miles in space. On September 16, they launched their most advanced electronic intelligence satellite, Cosmost 2,263 on a 545 mile orbit, joining the four others already on station. On September 17, they launched their next member of ocean surveillance satellite, with hyperspectral sensors and advanced lasers, building a network to track our Tridents.

Chapter 13:

Middle East Today

Behold, I will make Jerusalem a cup of trembling unto all the people round about, when they shall be in the siege both against Judah and against Jerusalem.

And in that day will I make Jerusalem a burdensome stone for all people: all that burden themselves with it shall be cut in pieces, though all the people of the earth be gathered together against it.

Zechariah 12:2, 3

The Middle East is changing so fast that this "update" will be, of necessity, obsolete by the time you have it in your hand. (This is why we publish a monthly intelligence newsletter.)[1]

Seven of Russia's largest military bases are located in the Middle East. And it is the caldron that will be the stage for the final showdown.

First, let's examine the broader horizon.

The International Arms Market

At the present time there are 22 Third-World countries developing ballistic missiles.

The SCUD-B is held by Afghanistan, Egypt, Iraq, Libya, Syria, Yemen, Iran and North Korea. Modified SCUD-C's have been shipped to Syria from North Korea. South Korea has sold 300 Scuds to Iran and Libya. North Korea also ships the *Taepo Dong* 1 and 2.[2]

China has the long range (1,500 mile range) CSS-2 *Dong Fen* missiles. They sold some to Saudi Arabia; there are 28 launching pads installed near al-Kharj, south of Riyadh.

Libya has developed the *Fateh*, (250 mile range).

Israel has the Jericho II (700 mile range), and the Jericho IIb (1,500 miles).

India has the *Agni* ballistic missile (1,500 mile range) (1989) and is developing one with a 2,500 mile range.

Pakistan has their *Hatf* II and III, plus longer range one under development.

Indonesia has the long range RX-250.

Taiwan has the *Tien Ma* (450 mile range).

Brazil has seven missiles under development including one with a 1,500 mile range.

Argentina has the Condor II (400 mile range); also, the short range Alacran.

Biological Weapons

The recent disclosures regarding the use of chemical and biological weapons by Iraq have highlighted another dimension of the terrors from the tensions in the Middle East. Some 10 countries are now believed to be involved in such development, and more than 30 agents have been identified for use in weapons, including anthrax, botulism, smallpox, hepatitis, yellow fever, and Lassa fever.

North Korea is the leader in developing biochemical warfare. They have cultured 13 kinds of bacteria including yersinia pestis, bacillus anthracis, vibrio cholera 01, salmonella typhi, and clostridium botulinum.

North Korea also has nine plants producing cyanic chloride, picric chloride, phenol chloride, and other chemical agents, with a production capacity of more than 5,000 tons annually. They are equipped with more than 1,000 poison-counteracting vehicles and 500 mobile detection units. Over the past 10 years they have conducted over 630 exercises.

Such weapons were banned under the Geneva Convention of 1925 and a further agreement in 1975. The U.S. Congress has now made it a criminal offence for any U.S. citizen to take part in a biological-warfare program. Certain chemical agents were also outlawed during Desert Storm, (such as CS gas, which apparently is now confined to special circumstances, such as the children and their parents at Waco).

Iran

Iran is the lead ally listed in Ezekiel 38,[3] and is now emerging as the dominant leader in the world of Islam. President Hashamir Rafsanjani, has announced his "Grand Design" to unite the entire Muslim world into an Islamic Crescent, from the 200 million Muslims in Indonesia in the Pacific, to Senegal and Mauritania on the Atlantic. He has already created an axis with Syria, and is attracting others.

Rafsanjani believes that "Islam has replaced Marxism as the ideology of the future," and that they soon will have the resources (both the oil revenues and nuclear weapons) to finally disconnect the Middle East from the traditional Judeo-Christian order of the West.

In October 1991, Dr. Madi Charan, for the General Command Headquarters of Iran, acquired three nuclear weapons for $150 million from the ICBM base at Simipolatinski in Kazakhstan. He also recruited a substantial number of scientists from Kurchitov (near Moscow) and multiple warhead specialists from Kazakhstan.

In November 1991, Iran's President Hashamir Rafsanjani called a council of his High Command[4] and announced, "The objective is to eliminate the west from the Middle East and to liberate Jerusalem."

Yeltsin has signed a military assistance treaty with Iran to back them in their ambitions.

Iran has spent more than $14 billion in the last three years on its air force.

Remember the 115 Iraqi planes fled to Iran during the Persian Gulf War? Iran has purchased spare parts as well as an additional 110 aircraft from Yeltsin: 12 Tuplev-22 ("Backfire") bombers;[5] 48 MIG-29 ("Fulcrum") interceptors; 24 MIG-27 ground attack aircraft; some MIG-31 ("Foxhound") fighters; and 2 IL-76 AWAC's. Price tag: $2.2 *billion*!

North Korea has shipped more than 100 Scud missiles to Iran, in addition to the 250 already received from China and Russia. North Korea may also be supplying its longer range *Taepo Dong* 1 and 2 ballistic missiles in the near future.[6]

China has supplied Iran with 38 warplanes, 10 ballistic missile systems (including 5 Silkworm systems), 400 tanks, and 400 medium-range 120mm and 122mm artillery pieces, as well as components and computerized machine tools to improve the accuracy of the North Korean Scud missiles already in its arsenal.

Iran has purchased seven nuclear warheads from Kurchitov (the nuclear stockpile near Moscow), and from Simipolatinski (the ICBM base in Kazakhstan). Yeltsin is now also installing two nuclear plants in Iran and a nuclear research facility at Isfahan.

CIA Director James Woolsey, before he resigned recently, indicated that there are now more than 7,000 nuclear scientists and engineers working in Iran. This is the largest pool of nuclear talent in the Islamic world.

Russian experts are continuing to build a nuclear complex in Iran, despite Washington's attempts to pressure Russia to cancel the $1 Billion project.[7] Russians have maintained that cancellation is "out of the question."

(Russia receives $500 million *per month* in aid from the International Monetary Fund.)

Iran's strategic naval focus appears to be on two of the objectives: the Red Sea (which passes over 25,000 ships per year) and the Strait of Hormuz in the Persian Gulf (which passes 25% of world's oil). The Iranian Port Sudan access, along with the annexation of Abu Musa Island in the Persian Gulf (and its control of the entrance through the Straits of Hormuz) has also put more focus on Iran's recent acquisition of the three Russian Kilo-class (diesel powered) submarines. They are also negotiating for two more.

Iran will be deploying Silkworms or CS-801 Sardine antiship cruise missiles on the Sirri Island, 45 miles off the Iranian coast in the Persian Gulf this year. Over a quarter of the world oil trade flows through the Straits of Hormuz.

NATO, at a private meeting in Brussels, acknowledged that they believe a nuclear confrontation in the Middle East is certain; it is only a question of timing.

They have even begun practicing. The current operating maneuvers[8] are now testing the latest scientific and technological advances. From satellite reconnaissance, we know that these exercises include amphibious operations under conditions of contamination, which divulges a strategic insight. Such operations would not be necessary against Israel. These training maneuvers reveal that Rafsanjani's strategy apparently includes the invasion of *Saudi Arabia*.

Why would Iran invade Saudi Arabia? Aren't they Muslim? Not exactly: they are Sunni, not Shi'ite. Furthermore, for Rafsanjani's goal of leading the *Islamic Crescent* of his "Grand Design," he needs to control both Mecca and Medina.

No wonder "Sheba and Dedan" are nervous.[9]

Iraq

Iraq was the cradle of the Shi'ite branch of Islam, with about 55% being Shi'ite, although Saddam Hussein and his cohorts, presently in control, are Sunni's. While not beloved in the West, he serves as a balance wheel between Iran and Syria.

Saddam Hussein had planned to again invade Kuwait and Saudi Arabia in September 1995, but called off the attack after two top aides defected to Jordan. Lt. General Hussein Kame al-Majid, Iraq's industry minister, his brother, Col. Saddam Kamel al-Majid, head of the President's elite corps of personal body guards, and their wives--both daughters of Saddam's--defected, highlighting instability in the innermost circle.

Lt. General Hussein Kamel al-Majid indicated that when the Gulf War began, Iraq was only three months away from testing its nuclear weapons.

Iraq now admits that there were five secret facilities producing a large stockpile of anthrax and botulinum toxin as well as three other types of poisons. During the Gulf War, more than 1,500 gallons of anthrax toxin was loaded into 50 bombs and 10 missile warheads. Nearly 3,000 gallons of Botulinum toxin, an agent that attacks the nerves and chokes its victims to death, was poured into 100 bombs and 15 missile warheads and sent to airfields.[10]

This may hold the explanation why 50,000 Gulf War veterans believe they suffer from symptoms from exposure to these chemical agents.

Iraq claims the agents were destroyed after the war.

One reason Saddam never used his biological weapons is that Washington had sent him veiled threats indicating that the U.S. would retaliate with nuclear arms if he did.[11]

The unfortunate failure of the U.S. to complete the task during Desert Storm has been ascribed to an overestimated fear of casualties, worry that a pro-Teheranian ruler would take over, but the inside word is that the big reason was the impending threat that Russia was about to enter the conflict directly.

Saddam Hussein's survival is amazing. It is particularly awesome thru Islamic eyes.

The Israeli's caught the consternation of the world press when their raid in 1981 knocked out the Osirak nuclear reactor near Baghdad, destroying Iraq's nuclear weapons capability. Where would we have been in the Persian Gulf War if they *hadn't?*

Before the Gulf War, Iraq had about 1.2 million men organized into seven corps and some 68 divisions: 12 Republican Guard Divisions, 6 armored, 3 mechanized infantry, and 47 infantry divisions. Iraq's armed forces had about 5,800 tanks, 5,100 armored personnel carriers, 3,850 artillery pieces, and 650 combat aircraft.

The allied forces destroyed around 3,850 tanks, 1,450 armored personnel carriers, 2,900 artillery pieces, 250 aircraft, and 150 naval vessels. About 15,000 Iraqis were killed, 100,000 deserted, and 86,000 were taken prisoner.

The result has left Saddam Hussein with an army of 400,000 men, organized into 29 divisions, most operating at about 70% capacity. He appears to have about 2,000 tanks, 3,000 armored personnel carriers, and 1,000 artillery pieces still operational. He still has most of his fleet of 600 helicopters, including 150 attack choppers. His airforce has about 150 modern aircraft out of about 300 remaining.

About 150,000 of Saddam Hussein's troops are located in the north to deal with the Kurds; about 50,000 in the south to deal with the Shi'ites. The 40,000 Republican Guard units are stationed in Baghdad.

Russia is pressing for a relief of the sanctions against Iraq in the hopes of collecting the $8 billion debt it owes Russia. Russia has supplied more than $20 billion to Iraq and Afghanistan over the past 18 months.

Babylon Being Rebuilt

From a Biblical point of view, our focus is 62 miles south of Baghdad, on a group of restorations known as Babylon. The Bible predicts that this ancient city is destined to be destroyed in the final confrontation.[12] It presently consists only of some ceremonial buildings, although Saddam Hussein has spent more than $900 million to restore them thus far, and has used them for affairs of state as early as 1987. They were not a military target. (On the military charts used during Desert Storm, they simply showed up simply as "numerous large buildings" along the River Euphrates, 14 miles southwest of Al Hillah.)

If we understand the Biblical passages correctly, this site is destined to rise to major prominence in the years ahead. It has a prophetic destiny to yet be destroyed as a major city in the future.

Syria

Syria is another aggressive antagonist of Israel, and is part of the axis with Iran's Grand Design.

Russia has supplied more than $21 billion in new advanced weapons to Syria over the past five years.

In a 27-page report to the House Foreign Affairs Committee, it has been estimated that Iraq has managed to reconstruct 80% of their military capability it possessed prior to Desert Storm. Iraq has rebuilt many of the weapons plants damaged during the air campaign; resumed production of weaponry at 40 major plants; returned to service 2,500 tanks and 250 combat aircraft, damaged or hidden during Desert Storm; and revived its clandestine network of undercover companies in Jordan, France, and Germany, to procure components for its weapons industries.

Assistant Secretary of State Robert Gallucci admitted that Iraq's nuclear weapons program is still very active, despite the ineffectual attempts to inspect and monitor Iraq by the International Atomic Energy Agency and the U.N.

Lebanon's Bekaa Valley is controlled by Syria and is the main center for cultivation of cannabis and opium poppies, producing 30 - 60 *tons* of heroin annually. The amount of land devoted to drug cultivation has increased by a factor of 10 since Syria seized the region in 1976. According to CIA sources, there is widespread Syrian army involvement in drug traffic from the Bekaa Valley. President Assad's brother, his defence minister, Mustafa Tlass, his domestic intelligence chief, General Ali Dubah, have all amassed huge fortunres from this drug trade. Drug funds also help Syria support the Shi'ite Hezbollah, and other groups who regularly attack Israel from Lebanon.

Turkish and Syrian officials are attempting to resolve their traditional differences in an attempt to promote a security agreement. Turkey is looking for Syria to deny support to the Kurdish Workers Party (PKK), battling to establish a separate state in southeast Turkey. Syria is looking for an improved sharing agreement of the waters of the Euphrates River, dammed by Turkey. This will be discussed in the next chapter.

Libya

There are 14 major Russian air bases in Libya alone, with more than 550 Russian combat aircraft. The Russians have more jets in Libya than the total combined air forces of England, West Germany, and France.

They also have prepositioned a staggering 16,000 tanks and armored cars in Libya, more than the combined tank forces of France, Britain, and Germany.

The key question is, why?

Israel

The home for Israel's strategic nuclear deterrent is at a missile base near Kefar Zekharya, in the Judean hills. Built in 1967, it is still undergoing expansion, according to satellite imagery from French and Russian satellites.

("I have reason to believe" that Israel had nuclear weapons available as early as the Six Day War in 1967. I wonder what would have happened if it lasted seven days?)

Don't underestimate the technology available in Israel. Israel Military Industries' pilotless *Delilah* unmanned air vehicle, first fielded in the 1980's, has a stealth coating to enable it to evade radars.[13] The Israeli's even have a holographic film in development to defeat *optically*-guided weapons.

The first explosive reactive armor system was produced by Rafael in Israel. (It is disturbing to know that the U.S. didn't have the technology to penetrate advanced Russian armor.[14] Fortunately, the Israeli's, and the Germans, can.)

The tragedy of the current so-called "Peace Negotiations" is that they are based on the presumption that reducing the land available to Israel will appease the Muslim antagonists. All that will do is eliminate the option of a *conventional* response to any threatened attack, and force them to resort to a nuclear alternative for Israel's survival--probably a *preemptive* one.

Terrorism

Iran funds more than $100 million a year to terrorist organizations.[15] There are now 30 schools in the Sudan, funded by Iran, for training terrorists for use in the U.S. and Europe. Some of these are being moved to Angola.

Terrorist groups currently operating out of Syria and Lebanon include: the Hamas, the Hezbollah, ("Party of God"), the Palestinian Islamic Jihad, the Abu Nidal Organization, the Popular Front for the Liberation of Palestine, the Democratic Front for Liberation of Palestine, the Popular Struggle Front, the Abu Musa Group, Al-Sa'iqa, the Kurdish Revolutionary

Workers' Party, the Armenian Secret Army for Liberation of Armenia, the Japanese Red Army, and many others.

Not the least of the potential nuclear threats are those of the terrorist groups. 19,000 Russian warheads are somewhere, but nobody is sure where.[16] Warehoused in as many as 100 sites, many are in temporary storage areas under army control. Some experts even estimate that tactical nuclear stockpiles could have as many as 43,000 warheads.[17] The controls and accountability for the enormous Soviet stockpile are ineffective and virtually nonexistent.[18] A large number of warheads and materials are on the black market.[19] Not a week goes by without an incident of someone being apprehended in an attempt to traffic in such strategic items.[20]

A group of terrorists would only have to smuggle into the country something about the size of a footlocker, and they then could plant a *nuclear device* in the World Trade Center, or a Federal Building in some city--wherever they felt they wanted to "make a statement." Now the Chechens are also suspected of seeking access to such devices.[21]

Notice that the PLO is not listed. They really don't speak for Israel's enemies. There are 10 Damascus-based Palestinian factions who oppose Arafat's policies, etc.

The "Peace Process"

The current PLO Accord, tragically, does little more than guarantee a military event. It is based on false premises:

1)   The PLO does not speak for Israel's enemies. The other groups are out to prove it.

2)   The Muslims insist on what Israel cannot yield: The issue is not the *size* of Israel; it is the *existence* of Israel that is the Islamic issue. They are committed to obtaining *all* of Palestine.

Today most jounalists and politians in the West are of the misguided opinion that as long as Israel withdraws from the "occupied territories," namely, Gaza, Judea and Samaria ("The West Bank") and the Golan Heights, there will be a chance for peace in the Middle East.

This view emerges from their false perception of the conflict as being basically over land--rather than the reality that what is being sought is the elimination of Israel from the map altogether. This is the same goal that preoccupied the Nazis in Europe.

During the Six Day War, Egyptian President Gamal Abdel Nasser was not commanding his army and soldiers to liberate Gaza and the "West Bank"--these were *already* in in Muslim hands (Egypt's and Jordan's). The goal was the destruction of the State of Israel in the name of Allah and Islam.

The PLO was formed in 1964, *three years before* the "West Bank" was lost in the Six Day War of self-defense. Rather than simply liberate the West Bank--which was already in Arab hands--the PLO was formed to "liberate" all of Palestine from Jewish sovereignty, as its name clearly implies.

If it had been a simple question of dividing up the land between two peoples--the Jews and the Arab Palestinians--then the Arabs had ample opportunity during 1947, when the United Nations resolution suggested just that: the partition of the land into states for the Arabs and the Jews. It was the Muslims, not the Jews, who refused to accept this partition plan because they wanted it all: Tel Aviv, Jaffa, Haifa... all of it.

The Middle East conflict has been falsely "sold" by the Muslims to a gullible world as though the Jews took Arab lands. In fact, the opposite is true. The Muslims declared war on Israel in 1948 because they wanted to have the land which had been set aside by the United Nations for the Jews, and that is why there has been war--and terrorist crimes--in the Middle east for almost 50 years.

The original land of the Palestine Mandate, set aside by the League of Nations and the Balfour Declaration for the Jews to establish their homeland, included the land both east and west of the Jordan River. However, this Jewish homeland was unilaterally carved up, by the British yielding to Arab pressure, with 75% of the area given to placate the Hashemite, King Faisal.

Even this was not enough for the Arabs: Israel had to be completely destroyed. (The joint territory occupied by their militant opponents is 614 times larger than what was left to Israel, twice the size of the United States.)

For those who fail to see the relevance of the Bible to these issues, it is provocative to note that Israel's enemies take it very seriously. In July 1982, the UN passed a resolution that the history related by the [Jewish] Bible be rewritten so that the Jews were left out of it.[22]

The raising of the Muslim expectations, along with the pressures continuing to weaken Israel, all lead to making an attack appear as a rational option for them.

Egypt

The absence of any mention of Egypt in Ezekiel 38. is surprising.   It is such a key player in so many prophetic passages. Perhaps Egypt is included in the "many other nations with thee."[23]   However, it appears surprising to some of us if this is to be viewed as a parallel passage to Daniel 11.   The placement of Ezekiel 38 will be explored in chapter 17.

Next, let's talk Turkey.

Endnotes:

1. There should be a gift certificate in this book for an introductory year's subscription to Personal UPDATE. If not, call us at 1-800-KHOUSE1, or write P.O. Box D, Coeur d'Alene ID 83816.

2. Janes' *Defense Publications*, an authoritative UK source, indicates that North Korea has a 5,500 mile missile under develoopment.

3. Ezekiel 38:5.

4. Present were Ali Akhbar Tukin, Commander of the Armed Forces; Mushin Reszi, Commander of the Republican Forces; Allah Ali Fallaheyan, Head of Intelligence; and Akhmad Kohmeni, head of the clandestine espionage network in Europe and the U.S.

5. The Tu-22-M3, incidentally, has little relationship to the traditional Tu-22. This advanced design has a 1370 mile operating range, and other capabilities. This totally new aircraft has been designated a variant of the Tu-22 to skirt arms treaty limitations.

6. *Aviation Week & Space Technology*, May 8, 1995, p.19.

7. Admitted Moscow's Deputy Atomic Energy Minister. *Wall Street Journal*, August 21, 1995.

8. Code named "*Falaq*-2", September 19, 1994.

9. Ezekiel 38:13.

10. "Baghdad's Dirty Secrets," *U.S. News & World Report*, September 11, 1995, p.41.

11. "Saddam Spills Secrets," *Time*, September 4, 1995.

12. Isaiah 13 & 14; Jeremiah 50 & 51; Revelation 17 & 18. For a full exploration of this topic, see *The Mystery of Babylon*, Koinonia House.

13. The Delilah resembles the U.S. Air Force AGM-86 air-launched cruise missile; nine feet long, can be launched from the ground, aircraft or ships. It has a coating of Signaflux, a blend of polyaniline and cyanate whiskers (microscopically thin strands of carbon-60 fiber whose electrical conductivity has been modified) to render it less detectable to radar.

14. The Russian anti-tank technology is also available on the international market. The 9K115 Metis has a range limit to 600 meters; the 9K111 Fkatoiya has a range to 2,000 meters; the 9k113 Konkurs, to 4,000 meters.

15. CIA Director R. James Woolsey, final briefing in his last day as Director, January 10, 1995.

16. *Los Angeles Times*, May 8, 1994. We now understand that these figures are low estimates.. *NY Times,* Oct 93: 47,000 warheads. The current Department of Defense estimates are about 43,000.

17. Bruce Blair, Brookings Institution, Washington D.C.

18. Even in the U.S., the Dept of Energy has conceded that it does not have an accurate reckoning of how much radioactive plutonium was produced *in the U.S.* during the Cold War years. (12/7/93: ± 1.2 metric *tons*!)

19. In Russia, over 3,000 officers are presently facing court-maritals on corruption charges.

20. Congressional hearings held in August 1995 concluded that neither Washington nor Moscow are effectively heading off the smuggling of weapons-grade material out of Russia.

21. A number of nuclear mines have been stolen are are feared as falling into their hands. (Intelligence Digest, July 21, 1995.)

22. Becker, Jillian, *The Rise and Fall of the PLO*, Weidenfeld and Nicolson, London, 1987, p. 173.

23. Ezekiel 38:6.

Chapter 14:

Meshech and Tubal Today

"The emergence of the Turkic world is one of the most significant developments of this century. A new continent called Eurasia has been born in the geographic space that stretches from the Adriatic Sea to the Great Wall of China. Eurasia is tantamount to the Turkic world."

--President Sulleyman Demirel

When the Russian ships cross the Dardanelles, put on your Sabbath garments--the Messiah is coming.

--Ancient Hebrew Proverb

In chapter 9, we identified Meshech and Tubal with modern day Turkey. With the decline of the Byzantine Empire in the 14th century, Turkish tribes in Anatolia established the Ottoman Empire which lasted until after World War I, when the modern state of Turkey was formed.

It is fascinating to observe the dramatic changes which are presently underway in this key link between Europe and Asia. Three major factors are bringing about a strategic change in the Middle East with regards to Turkey:

1)   The rejection by the European Suprastate of Turkey's application for full membership;

2)   The opening up of the Turkic world of Central Asia;

3)   The rise of Islamic fundamentalism in Turkey.

The Ataturk Legacy

In the years following World War I, Kemal Ataturk aggressively transformed Turkey from a theocratic autocracy into a Western-oriented democracy. In 1922, he abolished the Sultanate. In 1924, he abolished the Caliphate and the religious courts. In 1925 he made it illegal to wear the fez (which he regarded as a symbol of backwardness).

It is impossible for us in the West to appreciate the extent of his commitment to bring this ancient and proud people into the benefits of Western civilization.

Having rid Turkey of the shackles of Islamic repression, Ataturk proceeded to adopt Western ways. In 1925 Turkey adopted the Western calendar. In 1926, it adopted the Swiss civil code (and later the Iranian penal code). In 1928 the country switched from the Arabic of the Koran to the Latin alphabet. In 1931, it switched to the metric system. In 1934, all Turks were obliged to take a surname (Mustafa Kemal became Kemal Ataturk), and the women were given the vote.

Following World War II, Turkey joined all the main Western institutions: The UN in 1945; the IMF in 1947; the OECD in 1948; the Council of Europe in 1949; and NATO in 1951, and, after four years of application, received associate membership in the European Community in 1963.

Turkey has had a supporting role on NATO's southern flank, but in the Caucasus, Balkans and Mideast, Turkey's role is pivotal.

The European Rejection

A crisis began to loom as Turkey applied for full membership of the European Community on 14 April 1987. Although Turkey's associate membership agreement of 1963 specifically held out full membership as an eventual goal, and their application in 1987 was ahead of Austria, Finland, Sweden, and

Norway, whose applications have been accepted and expedited, it was quickly becoming apparent that they have been rejected by the new European Union.

It has become painfully obvious to them that Turkey is still viewed as a Middle Eastern nation with no business in the New Europe. This is a deep affront to a people who have, for 70 years, so categorically rejected their own past and culture in the hope of becoming Western. Their rejection has, understandably, changed their course and their strategy.

However, a new opportunity has been created by the Soviet break up. It is to turn back in the direction Islam. Left out in "Europe's hallway," Turkey is now on the road to becoming another member of the growing Muslim brotherhood.

The Emergence of Central Asia

The break up of the Soviet Union has released the five southern former republics, collectively referred to as Central Asia, as independent states. Four out of five of these former Soviet republics are Turkic-speaking.[1] (Tajikistan is the exception, speaking a Persian dialect).

President Sulleyman Demirel is now heading a drive to extend Turkish influence into the region.[2] It is significant that Demirel's "Eurasia" also includes Muslim Bosnia and Muslim Albania.

The Sword of Allah Returns

Islam has now again become a significant influence in Turkey, particularly through the Directorate of Religious

Affairs, which is attached to the Prime Ministry, and has substantial resources (including 90,000 civil service personnel) under its control.[3] It supplies imams (mosque prayer leaders) to every village or town; it writes the sermons these imams must preach; it organizes the pilgrimages to Mecca; it provides commentaries on religious themes, publishes the Koran and other works; pronounces judgements on religious questions; monitors mosque building; provides teachers and advisors to Turkish citizens living abroad, and helps oversee official religious ties with other countries.

Furthermore, the secondary education system, the Ankara University faculty, the police force, and the media, are all becoming increasingly Islamically controlled.

The Refah Party

The Refah Party (Refah means "welfare") is the rapidly emerging Islamic Party in Turkey. Its core values are xenophobia, chauvinism and anti-Semitism.

It is a crime in Turkey for a political party to advocate an Islamic state, so the Refah Party moves quietly. However, it already has 38 seats in the 450-member Parliament. It has won 16 of the 27 boroughs of Istanbul. Growing poverty, corruption scandals, and widespread disenchantment are all driving more and more voters into the arms of the Islamic party.

Not surprisingly, the Refah Party captured both Ankara and Istanbul, among 29 (of 79) major municipalities and 400 minor ones. Extrapolation of these results imply that they may capture 146 seats of the 450 in the next major election (1996), emerging as either a coalition partner or the major opposition party.

In July 1994, the appointment of Mumtaz Soysal as Turkey's foreign minister is significant since he is a long standing critic of the west and is even referred to in the German press as "Turkey's Zhirinovsky." (See chapter 15.)

The Islamic Crescent Grows

Beginning in December 1993, Iran, Syria and Turkey began banding together over fears of an independent Kurdistan in northern Iraq. It was through Iranian mediation that Turkey and Syria apparently signed a secret deal on cooperation, despite continuing differences over the sanzak of Alexandretta and the Euphrates.

The Kurds

Reports on the tensions in the Middle East and Central Asia also frequently mention the Kurds. Here, also, are some unique insights for the Biblically informed.

A People Without a Country

The Kurds live in contiguous areas of Iran, Iraq, and Turkey, with a dream of forming their own independent country of "Kurdistan." They number approximately 10 million, including those in Armenia and Syria. Unlike their Shi'ite Iranian neighbors, most Kurds are Sunni Muslims.

They have a traditional reputation for military prowess and have been successful mercenaries and professional soldiers in many armies. Saladin, the famed Kurdish warrior of the 12th century fought against Richard I of England in the Third Crusade, and created the Ayyübid Dynasty of Egypt (1169-1250 A.D.). Earlier there had been brief Kurdish dynasties in the 10th and 12th centuries.

The Kurds are a growing problem in the Muslim world. They have suffered a tradition of abuse and disenfranchisement in each of the countries they reside in.

Kurdish nationalism has been reflected in frequent uprisings against the Ottoman and Persian governments. After the first World War, the Treaty of Sèvres (1920) provided for an autonomous Kurdistan, but that treaty was never ratified. Uprisings in Iraq and in Iran have continued and the indigenous Kurdish population has continued in refugee/guerilla status throughout the region.

The Kurds of Iran

The Kurds appear to have descended from the Medes of ancient history who joined with the Persians and conquered Babylon in 539 B.C. This Medo-Persian Empire was the second of the four great empires predicted in the visions of Daniel chapters 2 and 7.

The Medes, an Indo-European people settled in the plateau land in northeastern Iran as early as the 17th century B.C. The ancient country of Media had their capital city at Ecbatana (modern Hamadan).

Cyrus II ("the Great") was part Persian and part Mede: his mother was Mandane, a daughter of Astyages, king of Media

(585-550 B.C.). When his father, Cambyses I, died in 559
B.C., Cyrus inherited the throne of Ansan and after unifying the
Persian people, he captured Astyages, took the capital city of
Ecbatana, and welded the Persians, with the Medes as honored
but subservient subjects, into a unified nation.

His capture of Babylon is detailed in Daniel chapter 5.
Daniel, although a Jew, later was appointed as the chief over the
hereditary Median priesthood known as the "Magi," a sect of
which had a prophetic role at the birth of Christ.[4]

The Medes disappear from history to re-emerge as the
mountain people known today as the Kurds.

The Kurds of Turkey

Turkey, too, is struggling with a militant Kurdish population, and is annoyed with Syria in not honoring their agreement
to liquidate the Kurdish rebel bases in Lebanon and Syria.
Israel has also opposed helping Turkey's actions against the
Kurdish rebels, and this is presently a barrier to better cooperation between the intelligence services of the two countries.

The Kurds of Iraq

The Kurds comprise approximately 18% of Iraq's population. Iraq created an admistrative district called Kurdistan
("Land of the Kurds") in 1974, comprising three northwestern
governorates of Iraq that border Turkey to the north and Iran to
the east.

Saddam Hussein has continued to oppress the Kurds in
Iraq, having even used chemical weapons against their civilian

population in recent years. No wonder the Kurds will enthusi-
astically participate in the ultimate destruction of Babylon.[5]

The Western air umbrella, which is based in Turkey and
guards a no-fly zone, protects the Kurds in northern Iraq from
attacks by Iraqi armed forces. Given Turkey's own hostility
toward an independent Kurdistan makes the continuation of this
accommodation doubtful. It is only a matter of time before
Saddam Hussein tries to reunite his country by force. Fighting
between the Kurdish groups that jointly rule Iraqi Kurdistan has
been encouraged Baghdad (and perhaps Ankara as well) to
forestall prospects for a truly independent Kurdistan.[6] Sources
in Iran report that Saddam Hussein is using the occasion to
move troops north towards the Kurdish enclave.

Central Asia

When the Soviet Union broke apart, roughly a third of the
Soviet strategic arsenal was left outside Russian borders in
three of the now "independent" republics, although under
undisputed Russian control: Ukraine, Belarus, and Kazakhstan.

Kazakhstan had 94 ballistic missiles (all SS-18 "Satans"),
40 strategic bombers, and 1260 nuclear warheads. It is also the
location of the Baikonur Cosmodrome, the former Soviet space
base. Russian and Kazakhstan are still disputing over the
control this 600-square mile facility in central Kazakhstan
which is still used for manned and unmanned missions. It has
launch pads for all of the primary vehicles used by the former
Soviet Union: Proton, Zenit, Soyuz, Energia, Molniya, Cyclone
and Vostok. If an agreement cannot be reached with Kazakhstan, Russia will have to transfer all its launch operations to
Plesetsk in northern Russia, which is already the world's busiest

spaceport. Its northern latitude—62.7° N—would result in some payload penalties, especially for the Mir-2 space station.

Summary

The world is more at risk now than ever before in history. The weapons are being distributed. The tensions increase. The stage is, indeed, being set for the final climax.

We have reviewed Magog and their allies. But what about Gog, their leader?

Endnotes:

1. The Turkic peoples are historically and linguistically linked with T'uchüeh, the name given by the Chinese to the nomad peoples who founded an empire stretching from Mongolia and the northern frontier of China to the Black Sea. The name originated from that of one of the khans of the Golden Horde who embraced Islam. They were all Muslim.

2. Much of this background has been excerpted from briefings of Intelligence International, Stoneyhill Centre, Brimpsfield, Gloucester, GL48LF, UK.

3. Dr. David Shankland, (acting Director of British Institute of Archeology), *Middle East Dialogue,* Oct 1994, Ankara.

4. For some surprising background, see *The Christmas Story*, Koinonia House.

5. Isaiah 13:17 alludes to "the Medes" as participants in Babylon's destruction.

6. See our updates in Jan and Feb 95 Newsletters.

    Much of this review has been excerpted from pulbications of Intelligence International Ltd., The Stoneyhill Centre, Brimpsfield, Gloucester, GL48LF, UK.

Chapter 15:

The Men
Who Would Be
Gog

*Thus the Lord showed me, and
behold a swarm of locusts were coming, and, behold, one of
the young devastating locusts was Gog, the King.*

Amos 7:1 (LXX)

*What to do? We have lost our way.
From afar, the Demon cries out,
He is leading us astray.*

-- Alexander Pushkin

Who is Gog? We have clear identification of the land of Magog, and from the context of the Ezekiel passage, Gog is obviously the leader of the people of Magog. In fact, by some renderings, he is the "Prince of Rosh, Meshech and Tubal." But who is he?

It is unusual, in the Bible, to have a key character emerge without a linkage of some kind to the background. Gog seems to suddenly show up from nowhere and doesn't seem to be clearly identified. A remarkable discovery has been noted that clarifies some key aspects of this fabled commander, but let's first examine some candidates.

The Gyges Conjecture

Some, in an attempt to relegate Ezekiel 38 to the historical past, have suggested that Gog is linked to the King of Lydia, Gyges (Gugu), who, incidentally, is credited with the invention of coinage.[1] Magog would be thus identified as Ma(t) Gugu, "land of Gyges."[2] Gog, thus, would refer to northern barbarians, Amrana Gagaya.[3]

Six inscriptions of Ashurbanipal (668-631 B.C.) relate to Gyges, who appealed to the Assyrians for aid in the face of the Cimmerian invasions.[4]

However, since the kingdom of Gyges did not extend to the areas of Meschech and Tubal, there is a significant problem in assuming that Gog is related to Gyges. Furthermore, the clear "end time" implications of the entire passage rules out historical conjectures as unfruitful.

The leader of Magog of the Ezekiel passage is yet to be revealed, and there are a number of potential candidates emerging on the horizon.

U.S.S.R. II?

It is widely recognized by informed observers that Boris Yeltsin is in trouble. Insiders at NATO Headquarters--and most intelligence services--suspect that, even now, he may not really be running things.

Public opinion polls indicate that nearly three-quarters of Russians feel that the dissolution of the U.S.S.R. was a mistake. The Communist Party of the Russian Federation, together with its Agrarian cohorts, holds a quarter of the seats in the State Duma. There is a coordinated effort to get the parliaments of all states to denounce the Beloveshskaya agreements, in which the presidents of Russia, Ukraine and Belarus agreed to dissolve the U.S.S.R. The growing popularity and political strength of neo-Communists suggests that their extremist agenda should be taken seriously.

In the theatre of Russian politics, the next act may be about to begin.

Mad Vlad?

Any discussion of candidates for Gog generally begins with Vladimir Zhirinovsky, the bombastic military extremist who has suddenly been propelled into the Russian political limelight. It has become fashionable in the Western press to portray him as buffoon or a madman due to his outlandish--yet frightening--public announcements, but it is a mistake to discount him.

His speeches, and headline grabbing antics, are skillfully designed for local consumption and are tailored to what the populace wants to hear. There are sources that have led us to understand that much of his material is written by the KGB.

Vladimir Zhirinovsky claims his long deceased father, Volf Andreyevich Zhirinovsky, was a jurist who died in a car accident 1946, shortly after Vladimir's birth. However, no records have been found for Volf Andreyevich Zhirinovsky. Documents do show a Andrei Vasilyevich Zhirinovsky who died of tuberculosis in August 1944, 18 months *before* Zhirinovsky's birth on April 25, 1946. A marriage registration shows that five months earlier, his mother married Volf Isakovich Eidelshtein, who was officially listed as Jewish. Vladimir apparently retained his Jewish name until he was 18. In the archives in Alma Ata, the capital of Kazakhstan, where Zhirinovsky was born and raised, his surname was listed on his birth registration as Eidelshtein ("precious stone"). Documents show he applied for, and received, permission to change his name to Zhirinovsky in June 1964, just before he moved to Moscow.

He apparently has had KGB ties from his student days at the Institute of Eastern Languages at Moscow University. According to a former senior officer in Soviet intelligence who was a double agent for the British, he was recruited by the KGB as an informer in Turkey in 1969. In the 70's, he reportedly worked for the KGB-backed Soviet Peace Committee in Moscow.

According to CIA sources, Zhirinovsky was also a member of a group called Shalom, which was outwardly pro-Jewish but set up by the Anti-Zionist League, a KGB front designed to create divisions among Soviet Jews.

Rising from anonymity as a lawyer at 47, and now bankrolled by Yeltsin's enemies and former KGB officials, Vladimir Volfovich Zhirinovsky now finds himself at the forefront of Russian politics.

Mein Kampf II

Zhirinovsky does not believe the current crises can be resolved in the domestic arena. Like Hitler, he sees the salvation of the nation in war and conquest. Zhirinovsky's recently published autobiography is called *The Last March to the South*.[5] One can't help but ponder the obvious parallels with Hitler's *Mein Kampf*.

Adolf Hitler wrote his political manifesto *Mein Kampf* ("My Struggle"), originally published in two volumes in 1925 and 1927. The first volume, *Die Abrechnung* ("The Settle-ment," or "Revenge"), treated Hitler's youth, his racist ideol-ogy, his anti-Semitism, and the need for German Lebensraum ("living space.") The second volume, *Die National-social-*

istische Bewegnung ("The National Socialist Movement"), outlined his political program. These were abridged into a single volume in 1930. Ultranationalistic, anti-Semitic, antidemocratic, and ultramilitaristic, it became, of course, the "bible" of the National Socialist Party (Nazi) of Germany's Third Reich.

One can't help but ponder the obvious parallels.

Just as with the Nazis in the 20's and 30's, ultranationlism exploits popular anger, fear and humiliation. Here in Russia we also have an empire in collapse, with hyperinflation, political chaos, and a once-proud nation suffering wounding blows to its pride.

In Weimar Germany in 1930 the people initially cast 18% of votes for the Nazis. Hitler and the Nazis took power three years later.

In the elections last December, Vladimir got 23%. (Yeltsin's party only got 15%. Recent polls continue to indicate further slides in Yeltsin's popularity.)

Hitler promised "*Lebensraum*" through the "*Drang Nach Osten*," the need for an eastward push to fulfill Teutonic destiny. In *the Last March to the South* Zhirinovsky targets the expansion of Russia to include the shores of the Mediterranean and the Indian Ocean.

Zhirinovsky has promised to destroy the Baltic nations of Estonia, Latvia and Lithuania with nuclear waste. He threatens to "nuke" the Japanese; overrun Afghanistan, invade Poland, Finland, and Germany, etc. Istanbul would also fall under

Russian control, fulfilling a traditional dream of the Czars. His office is decorated with a redrawn map which wipes out Austria, Slovenia, the Baltic states, the Czech Republic, and Bosnia. He also advocates the abrogation of the 1867 treaty deeding Alaska to the United States. He advocates the Russian conquest and control of the Persian Gulf and the Mediterranean.

Let him speak for himself.

"I see Russian soldiers preparing for their last march to the south. I see Russian commanders tracing on their maps the routes to the final destination. I see airborne planes in our southern regions. I see submarines coming to the surface at the shores of the Indian Ocean. I see our marines landing on these shores where the soldiers of the Russian army are already marching, and armored vehicles moving along with tremendous masses of tanks."

"This last redivision of the world has to be done as form of shock therapy--suddenly, swiftly, effectively."

"Our army is capable of this, all the more so since this is the only way of survival for the nation. And it will be the basis for the rejuvenation of the Russian army. The new military can be reborn only in the course of a military operation. An army degenerates in the barracks. It needs a goal, a great task. It needs to exercise its muscle. This would be purification for all of us. And the ringing of the Russian Orthodox bells on the shores of the Indian Ocean and the Mediterranean would be the sound of peace for the people of the region."

According to Zhirinovsky, the rest of the world would do precisely what it did when Hitler's armies marched around

Europe--nothing. This is what Russia's "nuclear shield" is all about: to ensure a new Munich on the part of the West. And, indeed, would any Western government risk annihilation for the sake of Turkey, Iran, . . . or Israel?

"Russia is a Superpower. We have enough nuclear weapons to destroy the world in about half an hour."

"I will beat the Americans in space. I will surround the planet with our space stations so that they'll be scared of our space weapons."

"Let all our enemies fear us. Let them squirm in Paris, London, Washington, and Tel Aviv."

Zhirinovsky believes that the European powers will do nothing to interfere with Russia's destiny because elimination of the "Moslem peril" will be in their interest. Only American will object, "but he won't interfere," he says, because "the alternative is too grave." (i.e., Russian nuclear weapons and missile defenses.)

The Clock Continues

It appears to be 1930, Weimar time.

Anyone who doubts that antidemocratic forces now dominate the Russian Parliament should reflect on the 253-67 vote in the Duma granting amnesty to those who tried to overthrow Boris Yeltsin. Respectable reformers, like Yegor Gaidar the leading reformer, and Prime Minister Viktor S. Chernomyrdin, the leading proponent of slow-paced reform, were left in the dust.

Meanwhile, Mad Vlad has recently been promoted to the rank of Lieutenant-Colonel in the reserves. This is viewed by many as a signal to the army for support. His 1993 election manifesto was clearly not his own unaided work; it was designed and written by his backers in the security forces.[6]

Meanwhile, despite a disastrous economy and continuing pleas for Western economic aid, Russia continues to modernize its nuclear forces. Why?

It takes substantial background for any attempt to competently analyze the "theatre" of Russian politics. However, it is a serious mistake to write-off Zhirinovsky. He is NATO's worst nightmare.

General Lebed

Another potential savior has emerged on the Russian scene. Worshiped with a fanatical zeal by the Russian 14th army, this hero of the Afghan war is consistently ranked as the most popular military man in the country. Lt. General Alexander Lebed has used his immense popularity as a platform for scathing attacks on the country's top politicians and bureaucrats. He has openly criticized his military superiors, espoused the idea of a military dictatorship, called for an expanded army, and appears to be courting a political career.

He has noted, "What's wrong with a military dictator? In all of its history, Russia has prospered under the strictest control. Consider Ivan the Terrible, Peter the Great, Catherine the Great, or Stalin."

He could be the dream candidate: a high profile outsider with strong nationalist credentials, untainted by mainstream politics, and bolstered by a reputation for incorruptibility and blunt honesty. In some recent surveys, General Lebed is ranked well ahead of Vladimir Zhirinovsky.

And never underestimate the role of the Russian army in Russian politics.

The Return of the Czar?

Yeltsin published a Presidential decree on December 1, 1993, officially replacing the familiar Soviet Hammer and Sickle with what some people consider the most unlikely symbol possible: the Romanov two-headed eagle is now the seal of the new Russia.

Facing east and west, the two headed eagle has been a symbol of the Russian Czars since the 15th century. This ancient insignia renewed its appearance on government buildings January 1, 1994.

The golden two-headed eagle was the emblem of the Byzantine Empire. Russia's Czar Ivan III ("The Great") adopted it after marrying the niece of the last Byzantine emperor in 1472. The version now adopted is similar to the one used by Peter the Great, with three crowns, an orb in one claw, and a scepter in the other. On the eagle's breast is the image of a rider on a white horse.

(It is intended to be St. George, the dragon slayer, the traditional herald of Moscow. Its similarity to the first of the Four Horsemen of the Apocalypse is provocative.[7])

The Romanov double eagle was used until 77 years ago when Czar Nicholas II, and his family, Russia's last reigning royalty, were executed by the Bolsheviks in July of 1918.

The adoption of this symbol was repeatedly rejected by the conservative Parliament until it was disbanded. The new legislature is now known by the pre-revolutionary name of the "Duma," the label used during the reign of the Czars.

Grand Count Vladimir Kirillovich, a Romanov and second cousin to Czar Nicholas II, died in 1992 at the age of 74. What is remarkable is that permission was granted by Yeltsin to have him buried in St. Isaac's Cathedral in St. Petersburg. This is an imperial honor that was previously unthinkable.

Grand Count Kirillovich had a great grandson, 14 year old Count Georgii Romanov, who lived in Madrid with his mother, Maria. When Yeltsin visited Spain last year he secretly visited young Count Georgii. Since then, the young Count has been enlisted in St. Petersburg's Nachimov Naval Academy[8] (which, thus, also grants him citizenship). Naval background and training has been the traditional path for training of the previous Czars.

Yeltsin may be planning to establish a constitutional monarchy as a way out of his present difficulties. A thousand-year-old monarchy would give Yeltsin's regime more legitimacy than three years of a "democracy" that is increasingly viewed as a failure. Yeltsin would, it is assumed, serve as his regent.

It is believed that both the Army and the Russian Orthodox Church would give their enthusiastic support, thus undermining both Rutskoi and Zhirinovski, Yeltin's main political rivals.

A fascinating alternative. Let's watch and see.

Gorbachev?

Gorbachev has announced his intention to run for Russia's presidency in 1996. This is surprising since his popularity among Western liberals is not matched in Russia where he is not admired.

It now appears that the famed "coup" of July 1991, which put Yeltsin in power was actually planned by Gorbachev, together with the coup "hard liners" including Vladimir Kryuchkov, KGB chairman, and Soviet Defense Minister Dmitri Yazov. All eight coup leaders have been released and pardoned. In interviews with the leading Canadian newspaper, the *Toronto Star*, each of them admitted that Gorbachev planned the coup with them for three weeks prior to his staged "arrest."

We understand that the papers for the Gorbachev Foundation were filed with the California Secretary of State's office in April 1991--four months *before* the pseudo-coup.[9]

Mikhail Gorbachev has received more than $300 million from the Rockefeller and Mellon Foundations to establish his private foundation to prepare the way "for world peace." German Chancellor Helmut Kohl arranged to provide another $100 million in support from German industrialists.

On October 19, 1994, Mikhail Gorbachev presented the "Final Report of the Global Security Project" to the Council on Foreign Relations in New York. This "Final Report" advocated complete elimination of nuclear weapons, global gun control, and drastic strengthening of the authority of the United Nations through regional security institutions. "Public participation" under this system would consist merely of an opportunity to ratify the UN's dictatorial decisions.[10]

Is he being groomed for a broader global role?

Other Candidates

There are other potential candidates and rivals to Boris Yeltsin. Alexander Rutskoi, and others, are often mentioned. It is also likely that a "dark horse" candidate might yet emerge to dominate the scene.

But clearly the current turmoil and disillusionment creates an ideal environment for a despotic leader to take charge. In recent surveys of political and media experts, there is a wide-spread expectation that a dictatorship will be established in Russia, and few believe Russia's problems can be solved without "authoritarian interference."

1996 is shaping up to be a pivotal year: there will be a watershed election in the United States; there will be an election for the leadership of Russia; there will be an election for the president of the European Union; there will be an election in Israel (if not sooner); and Jerusalem is on the "Peace" agenda.

And the positioning for each of these has already begun.

DemaGog or Demigod?

The sudden appearance of "Gog" in the Ezekiel text, without any apparent background from other passages, has puzzled commentators for centuries.   From the context, it is clearly the title of the leader of the people of the land of Magog. Still, it seems inconsistent with God's established style to have such a key figure emerge in the text without a linkage of some sort.

There is, however, a provocative reference that has been widely overlooked in the Book of Amos. The traditional rendering of Amos 7:1 reads as follows:

> *Thus hath the Lord God shewed unto me; and, behold, he formed grasshoppers in the beginning of the shooting up of the latter growth; and, lo, it was the latter growth after the king's mowings.*
>
> Amos 7:1 (KJV)

Our English Bible takes its translation from the Masoretic text, a 9th century source. However, an earlier translation of the Old Testament into Greek, known as the Septuagint, embodies a different rending of Amos 7:1:[11]

> *Thus the Lord showed me, and behold a swarm of locusts were coming, and, behold, one of the young devastating locusts was Gog, the King.*
>
> Amos 7:1 (LXX)

The Septuagint apparently drew upon other texts in translating the Hebrew of Amos 7:1.[12] (Subtle alterations or corruptions in the Hebrew can frequently yield substantial differences in meaning.)[13]

The identification of Gog as the king of the locusts would have profound implications. Proverbs 30:27 reveals that the "the locusts have no king," implying that the "locusts" of Amos 7 are not intended to be *natural* locusts, but an idiom for something else.

We encounter a similar passage in Revelation chapter 9 where locusts there are described as having a king, and so are clearly a *demon* host.[14]

The passage in Amos 7:1 suggests that *Gog* is the king of the demon locusts, and this would put an entirely new light on the Gog of Ezekiel 38 and 39. (Incidentally, the Sumerian word *gug* means darkness.[15])

A Trip to Hal's Study

As an interesting sidelight on this issue, when I first stumbled on this I was, frankly, amazed. My friend Hal Lindsey and I each maintain substantial personal libraries on prophecy in general, (and Ezekiel in particular) and I was stunned that I hadn't come across this before.

I scooped up my notes and went over to Hal's home, and we spent until 3:00 A.M. in his library going over his extensive sources to be sure of our grounds. And, indeed, it all checked out.

I personally was stunned that a verse like this had apparently been overlooked for so many centuries! Hal wasn't surprised at all. He said, "Chuck, this is simply an example, in itself, of prophecy being fulfilled":

> *But thou, O Daniel, shut up the words, and seal the book, [even] to the time of the end: many shall run to and fro, and knowledge shall be increased.*
>
> Daniel 12:4

Some people view the "knowledge shall be increased" as applying to knowledge in general--and, indeed, that certainly is true. They say that mankind's knowledge doubles every ten years. (Which means that half of all that we know emerged in the past ten years!) The "knowledge explosion" is the subject of many papers and books.

However, the strict application of this passage refers to knowledge of the Biblical text, and in understanding of the Word of God.

There is a reference to Gog and Magog leading a rebellion after the Millennium[16] which also has puzzled commentators. For Magog to reappear later is no surprise--it is a nation, a people. But for the leader Gog to reappear has been a dilemma. As the title of a demon king, however, the riddle is more easily resolved.[17] The placement of the Ezekiel passage will be explored in chapter 17.

But the issue of timing has far deeper implications. The next section will explore these.

Endnotes:

1. Tom Jones, *Paths to the Ancient Past,* Free Press, NY, 1967; p 70-96.

2. H. L. Ellison, "Gog and Magog," *Illustrated Bible Dictionary,* Ed. N. Hillyer, Inter-Varsity, Leicester, 1980, vol 1, pp. 573-574.

3. W. F. Albright, *Yahweh and the Gods of Canaan,* Doubleday, Garden City NJ, 1968, p.16.

4. D.D. Luckenbill, ed. *Ancient Records of Assyria and Babylonia,* Univesity of Chicago, Chicago, 1927, vol 2, pp.351-352.

5. Владимир Жириновский, Посдеаний Бросок На Юг, Москва, 1993.

6. *Intelligence Digest*, 14 April 1995.

7. Revelation 6:2.

8. *Moskovskie novosti*, No. 37.

9. McAlvany Intlligence Advisor, March 1995. (P.O. Box 84904, Phoenix AZ 85071.

10. "Gorbachev's Global Blueprint," The New American, December 12, 1994.

11. Rahlfs, Alfred, ed. *Jd Est Vetus Testamentum Graece IVXTA LXX Interpretes,* Vol 2., Privileg, Wurtt, Bibelanstalt, Stuttgart, 1935; F.W. Gingrich and Frederich Danker, *A Greek-English Lexicon of the New Testament and other Early Christian Literature,* University of Chicago Press, Chicago & London, 1957.

12. Hatch, Edwin, and Redpath, Henery A., *Concordance to the Septuagint and the Other Greek Versions of the Old Testament,* Akademische Druck-U-Verlagsanstalt, Graz, Austria,, 2 vols., 1954 (1897). The versions referenced are Codex Alexandrinus A, Codes Vaticanus B, Codex Siniaticus S, and Sixtine Edition of 1587 R. "When no variant is mentioned it may be understood that the four texts, or such of them as contain the passage, agree; or that the variants are unimportant." No variant of Amos 7:1 is mentioned.

13. גֵּזִי "mowing", vs. גּוֹג, "Gog."

14. Revelation 9:3ff. Note v. 11.

15. John W. Wevers, *Ezekiel, The New Century Bible Commentary,* Thomas Nelson and Sons, 1969, p. 199.

16. Revfelation 20:8.

17.   The reader is encouraged to also do a careful study of Daniel 10 to more fully
       appreciate the invisible powers behind each of the major governments on the Planet
       Earth.

Section V

The Timing

Behold ye among the heathen, and regard,
and wonder marvellously: for I will work a work in
your days which ye will not believe, though it was to
told you.

Habakkuk 1:5

Chapter 16:

Israel:
God's Timepiece

Red sky at night: Sailors' delight.
Red sky in the morning: Sailor take warning.
O ye hypocrites, ye can discern the face of the sky; but can ye
not discern the signs of the times?

Matthew 16:2, 3

Surely the Lord God will do nothing,
but he revealeth his secret
*   unto his servants the prophets.*

Amos 3:7

I srael is the lens through which the Bible presents both the past and the future. The entire history of Israel is an astonishing testimony to the supernatural origin of the Bible. The greatest miracle is before our very eyes: the Jew.

The regathering of Israel into their own homeland--the second time--is the key to understanding the times in which we live.[1]

There are many incredible examples we could select to demonstrate how God has repeatedly authenticated His messages through fulfilled prophecy regarding Israel. However, the last four verses of Daniel chapter 9 contain the most amazing passage in the Bible! It will not only demonstrate the astonishing reality that the Bible details history in advance, this passage also happens to be the key to all end-time prophecy.

Daniel was part of the Old Testament, and, as such, was translated into Greek as part of the Septuagint translation of the Hebrew Scriptures in 270 B.C. Although Daniel is one of the most authenticated books of the Bible, this simplifying observation will serve to establish the existence of the book long before the events it predicts.

The Confidential Briefing

Four disciples came to Jesus privately for a confidential briefing about His Second Coming. His response was so important that it is recorded in three of the Gospels.[2] In this briefing, Jesus highlighted this very passage in Daniel 9 as the key to prophecy.[3]

Daniel was deported as a teenager and then spent the next 70 years in captivity in Babylon. He was reading the prophecies of Jeremiah[4] from which he understood that the 70-year period that had been predicted was about to end, and so he committed himself to prayer. During his prayer, the Angel Gabriel came to him and gave him the most remarkable prophecy in the Bible. The last four verses of Daniel 9 are the famed "Seventy Week Prophecy" of Daniel.

The Seventy Weeks

The last four verses of Daniel 9 also highlights the fourfold structure of the passage:

9:24 The Scope of the entire prophecy;
9:25 The 69 Weeks;
9:26 An Interval between the 69th & 70th Week
9:27 The 70th Week

(The key to understanding this passage is to recognize that the 70 "Weeks" are not all contiguous, and that there is an explicit interval between the 69th and 70th Weeks.)

Verse 24: The Scope

Seventy weeks are determined upon thy people and upon thy holy city, to finish the transgression, and to make an end of sins, and to make reconciliation for iniquity, and to bring in everlasting righteousness, and to seal up the vision and prophecy, and to anoint the most Holy Place.

Daniel 9:24

Seventy *shabu'im* (sevens, or "weeks") speaks of weeks of years. This may seem strange to us as Gentiles, but the Hebrew traditions have a week of days, a week of weeks (*shavout*), and a week of years.[5] Seventy sevens of years are determined, or reckoned (*hatak*), upon Daniel's people and the city of Jerusalem. Notice that:

1) The focus of the passage is on the *Jews*, not the Church nor the Gentile world.

Also,

2) The six major items listed have *yet to be completed*:

    1) to finish the transgressions;
    2) to make an end of sins;
    3) to make reconciliation for iniquity;
    4) to bring in everlasting righteousness;
    5) to seal up (close authority of) the vision;
    6) to anoint the *Godesh Godashim,* the Holy of Holies.

The fact that not all of these have yet been fulfilled in 2,000 years also demonstrates that the time periods are not contiguous.

360 Day Years

All ancient calendars were based on a 360-day calendar: Assyrians, Chaldeans, Egyptians, Hebrews, Persians, Greeks, Phoenicians, Chinese, Mayans, Hindus, Carthaginians, Etruscans, Teutons, etc. All of these calendars were originally based on a 360-day year; typically, twelve 30 day months.

In ancient Chaldea, their calendar was based on a 360-day year and it is from this Babylonian tradition that we have 360 degrees in a circle, 60 minutes to an hour, 60 seconds in each minute, etc.

In 701 B.C., all calendars appear to have been reorganized.[6] Numa Pompilius, the 2nd King of Rome, reorganized the original calendar of 360 days per year, by adding five days per year. King Hezekiah, Numa's contemporary, reorganized his Jewish calendar by adding a month each Jewish leap year (on a cycle of 7 every 19 years.[7])

In any case, the Biblical calendar, in both Genesis and Revelation, uses a 360-day year.[8]

Verse 25: The 69 Weeks

Know therefore and understand, that from the going forth of the commandment to restore and to build Jerusalem unto the Messiah the Prince shall be seven weeks, and threescore and two weeks: the street shall be built again, and the wall, even in troublous times.

Daniel 9:25

Thus, Gabriel gave Daniel a mathematical prophecy:

(7 + 62) weeks, times 7 years/week,
times 360 days/year = <u>173,880 days</u>

173,880 days would occur between the commandment to rebuild Jerusalem until the presentation of the *Meshiach Nagid.* The trigger, the authority to rebuild the city of Jerusalem, was the decree of Artaxerxes Longimanus, given on March 14, 445 B.C.[9]

The target to complete the 69 weeks was the presentation of the *Meshiach Nagid*, the Messiah the King.[10] But just when was Jesus presented as a *King?*

On several occasions in the New Testament, when they attempted to take Jesus as a King, He invariably declined, "Mine hour is not yet come."[11]   Then one day, He not only permits it, He *arranges* it.

The Triumphal Entry

Jesus deliberately arranged to fulfill Zechariah 9:9.

Rejoice greatly, O daughter of Zion; shout, O daughter of Jerusalem: behold, thy King cometh unto thee: he is just, and having salvation; lowly, and riding upon an ass, and upon a colt the foal of an ass.

Zechariah 9:9

This was the only day He allowed them to proclaim Him as a King.[12] You and I might not recognize the Scriptural significance of what is known as the "Triumphal Entry" in a casual reading. However, whenever there is a danger of us missing a subtlety, the pharisees come to our rescue! Their response always underscores a significance we would otherwise have missed.

The enthusiastic disciples were declaring Jesus as the Messiah with Psalm 118.[13] When the pharisees expressed their concern over the apparent blasphemy, Jesus declared:

"I tell you that, if these should hold their peace, the stones would immediately cry out."
                                                    Luke 19:40

This was the 10th of Nisan,[14] or April 6, 32 A.D.[15] When you convert the Hebrew text into the terms of our calendar, we discover that there were *exactly 173,880 days* between the decree of Artaxerxes and the presentation of the "Messiah the King" to Israel! Gabriel's prophecy given to Daniel five centuries before--and translated into Greek three centuries earlier--was fulfilled to the exact Day!

This precise anticipation of historical details is one of the most dramatic demonstrations of the deity of Jesus Christ, the Messiah of Israel. Incredible!

Whenever we take a tour to Israel, I point out the best bargain in Israel. When we take them to the Mount of Olives, where there is great photo opportunity overlooking the Temple Mount, we usually walk down the very road that goes from Bethany down to Gethsemane--the road that Jesus rode the donkey on. As we walk, I suggest that everyone pick up a rock along the way and put in their pocket. When they back home, they are to mount it on a piece of wood as a conversation piece for their den, living room, or office. When people ask what it is, you simply explain, "That's one of the stones that didn't cry out!" And you get to tell them the whole story. After all, they brought it up.

(A descriptive chart of this famous prophecy is on the next page.)

What is also shocking is that Jesus held them *accountable* to recognize *this day*. He predicted that Jerusalem would be destroyed because they didn't recognize this specific day that Daniel had predicted.[16]

> *And when he was come near, he beheld the city, and wept over it, Saying, If thou hadst known, even thou, at least in this thy day, the things which belong unto thy peace! but now they are hid from thine eyes.*
> *For the days shall come upon thee, that thine enemies shall cast a trench about thee, and compass thee round, and keep thee in on every side, And shall lay thee even with the ground, and thy children within thee; and they shall not leave in thee one stone upon another; because thou knewest not the time of thy visitation.*
>
> Luke 19:41-44

But there's more.

The Seventy Weeks of Daniel

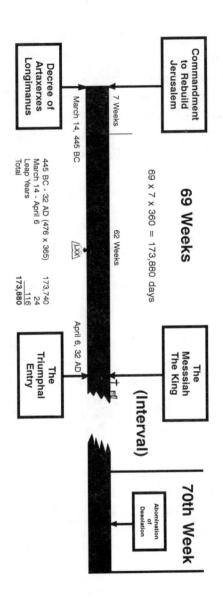

Verse 26: The Interval

> *And after threescore and two weeks shall Messiah be cut off, but not for himself: and the people of the prince that shall come shall destroy the city and the sanctuary; and the end thereof shall be with a flood, and unto the end of the war desolations are determined.*
>
> Daniel 9:26

Verse 26 deals with events *after* the 62 weeks (therefore, after the earlier seven, making it *after* a total of 69 weeks), and yet *before* the 70th week, which will be dealt with in verse 27. It is important to recognize that there are specific events specified *between* the 69th and 70th week, and, thus, not all the weeks are contiguous.

One of the events is that the Messiah shall be "cut off" (*karat*, execution; death penalty). It is a surprise to many to discover that the Old Testament *predicts* that the Messiah of Israel is to be *executed*.[17]

Another event which intervenes between the 69th and 70th week is that the city and the sanctuary would be destroyed. Indeed, as Jesus had predicted, 38 years after the end of the 69th Week, in 70 A.D., Titus Vespasian and the 5th, 10th, 12th, and 15th Roman legions laid seige to the city and slaughtered more than a million inhabitants.

Inadvertently, the interior of the Temple caught fire, the extensive gold coverings and fixtures had melted, and it was subsequently taken apart stone by stone to recover the gold. The specific prediction of Jesus was precisely fulfilled.

While there are specific events that required at least 38 years between the 69th and 70th Weeks of Daniel, this interval has now lasted more than 1,900 years thus far.[18] This interval is a period of national blindness for Israel[19] and the period that includes the Church, a mystery kept hidden in the Old Testament.[20] It seems that the Lord deals with Israel and the Church *mutually exclusively*. (A chess clock is an analogy: one clock is stopped while the other is running.)

The evidence is accumulating that this interval may be about over, and the famed 70th Week is about to begin.

Verse 27: The 70th Week

> *And he shall confirm the covenant with many for one week: and in the midst of the week he shall cause the sacrifice and the oblation to cease, and for the overspreading of abominations he shall make it desolate, even until the consummation, and that determined shall be poured upon the desolate.*
>
> Daniel 9:27

This is the final, climactic verse of the series. The first issue is to understand who the "he" is. The pronoun always refers to its immediate antecedent: here, the "prince that shall come" of verse 26. This is one of 33 allusions to this coming world leader in the Old Testament; he also has 13 allusions in the New Testament. He is commonly referred to as the "Antichrist."[21]

He, "the prince that shall come," will enforce a covenant with "the many" (an idiom for Israel) for the remaining seven years which make up the 70th Week.[22] He will violate this covenant in the "midst of the week" and the two halves of this seven-year period constitute the most documented period of time in the entire Bible. These periods are referred to as 3½ years,[23] 42 months,[24] 1260 days,[25] a half-week,[26] and time, times, and dividing of time.[27] ("Time" is singular; "times" is a dual; and "the dividing of time" is an idiom for a half; thus, 3½ years.)

The Abomination of Desolation

In His prophetic briefing, Jesus highlighted "the Abomination of Desolation" as the key milestone in end-time prophecy.[28] Such an event had occurred only once before in history. In 167 B.C., Antiochus IV ("Epiphanes") desecrated the Temple, and erected a pagan idol in the Holy of Holies.[29] This outrage incited the Maccabbean Revolt, which succeeded throwing off the yoke of the Selelucid Empire and then subsequently rededicating the Temple. This rededication is still commemorated by the Jews each year at Chanukah.[30]

This historical event occurred two centuries earlier, but provides the understanding of what Jesus was predicting would happen again in the future. It is this event that the "Prince that shall come" will stage in the "midst of the week." The Apostle Paul also detailed this event.[31]

Each of these references clearly requires the presence of a Temple in Jerusalem. There has been none since the destruction of 70 A.D. One of the many reasons it appears we are nearing the 70th Week is that preparations to rebuild the Temple have begun. (This will be discussed further in chapter 18.)

The Great Tribulation

From the "Abomination of Desolation" in the middle of the week until the end--which climaxes with the Second Coming of the Lord--is a period Jesus called "the Great Tribulation."[32] (Note that this is 3 1/2 years, not seven, as is so often assumed.)

Revelation chapters 6 thru 19 are essentially an elaboration of the events during the "70th Week" of Daniel 9.[33]

These views are not free of controversy, but are consistent with a strict interpretation of the Scriptures and the views of the early church.

Replacement Heresy

There are some who have confused the role of Israel and the Church, but that clear distinction is of paramount importance if one is to understand God's unique dealings with both.

There are some who believe that, because Israel rejected her Messiah, she forfeited the promises in the Old Testament and they now devolve upon the Church. The problem with this view is that the promises in question were *unconditional*; Israel couldn't forefeit them if she tried. This view denies Israel her place in God's program.

This view proved tragic for the Jews as it led to the Holocaust in Europe.[34] It also proved tragic for the Church since numerous heresies emerge by confusing the two, and assuming that the Church "replaces" Israel.[35] In Paul's definitive statement of Christian doctrine, the Book of Romans, he spends three chapters (9, 10, and 11), emphasizing that God is not through with Israel, and that Israel will yet be the primary "player" in the final climax.

The amillennial replacement theory has diverted many from the reality of God's revealed plan for history.

Upon the "conversion" of Constantine, his Edict of Toleration led to the declaration of Christianity as the official state religion of the Roman Empire in 325 A.D. As one can easily imagine, the view that Jesus Christ was destined to literally return to the Earth to defeat evil governments and rule a political kingdom was not popular with the Roman leadership.

Despite the messianic destiny clearly portrayed in the Old Testament, the promise of David's Throne confirmed to Mary, and the 1,000-year ("Millennial") reign prophesied in the Book of Revelation, Origen and others began to allegorize these passages and de-emphasized their literal significance. They preferred to view this "reign" in metaphorical terms rather than literally.

Augustine adopted this allegorical, or symbolic, "amillennial" view, which then became the dominant view of the Roman Catholic Church.

The Protestant Reformation, with its "back to the Bible" emphasis, dealt aggressively with the issues of salvation by faith, and other crucial doctrines, but the Protestant reformers failed to adequately challenge the eschatological[36] views of the medieval church. Thus, the "amillennial" views--and their associated "post-tribulation" views--have continued as a dominant perspective of many of the mainline Protestant denominations.

Many writers, including the great scientist and mathematician Sir Isaac Newton, continued to advocate a literal view of prophecy. Throughout the Bible, the people in the text invariably understand the prophecies they are reading literally.[37]

Since the "pre-millennial pre-tribulation" view was widely popularized by John N. Darby in 1820,[38] many, unfamiliar with the views held by the early church, ascribe the origin of these views to Darby; however, careful scholarship will show that these views are consistent with earliest records.[39]

The Big Surprise

We can't help but make "linear" assumptions in what is manifestly a nonlinear world. We always assume that things will remain the same as they have been. In the natural world, we never expect earthquakes, fires, floods, or other natural disasters. Yet they happen.

In the political world, there are also surprises. The Berlin Wall. The collapse of the Soviet Union.

In our personal, financial, or medical world, it is the same. We never expect the "unexpected." Yet it comes upon us, nevertheless.

Of all of the disruptions from God's interventions into human history, there is one yet coming that is more preposterous, more difficult to fathom, than any before it--even more than the flood of Noah.

It is the sudden *removal* of the Church,[40] leaving the people of this world . . . *to themselves*! Mankind is desperately pursuing a world without the God of the Bible--and He will let them have exactly what they want.

One of the most controversial aspects of the 70th Week is the timing of the "Rapture" (Greek, *harpazo*, Latin, *rapturo*), or "snatching out" of the Church.[41] Here is an analysis which we hope will be helpful:

1) 70th Week is *defined* by the enforcement of a covenant by the Coming World Leader.[42]

2) This Leader cannot enforce the covenant until *after* he attains the power to do so.

3) He cannot even appear until *after* the Restrainer (the Holy Spirit as He indwells the Church) is removed.[43]

4) Therefore, the rapture of the Church *precedes* (by an indeterminate amount) *the entire 70th Week*, not just the Great Tribulation.

This is why the allusion to Israel as "my people"[44] is so significant. This implies that the passage deals with events *after* the Church has been removed.[45]

With this background, just where does the invasion of Ezekiel 38 fit in? This is the subject of our next chapter.

Endnotes:

1. The first regathering was after the Babylonian captivity. The second time is now ocurring. Isaiah 11:11.

2. Matthew 24 & 25; Mark 13 & 14, and Luke 21 & 22.

3. Matthew 24:15.

4. Daniel 9:2; Jeremiah 25:11, 12.

5. Genesis 29:26-28; Leviticus 25, 26. A sabbath for the land ordained for every week of years: Leviticus 25:1-22; 26:33-35; Deuteronomy 15; Exodus 23:10, 11. Failure to keep the sabbath of the land was basis for their 70 years captivity: 2 Chronicles 36:19-21.

6. A fascinating conjecture as to the cause of this calendar change is detailed in *Signs in the Heavens,* a briefing package exploring the "long day" of Joshua and the possible orbital antics of the Planet Mars.

7. The 3rd, 6th, 8th, 11th, 14th, 17th and 19th are leap years, where the month Adar II is added. Arthur Spier, *The Comprehensive Hebrew Calendar*, Feldheim Publishers, Jerusalem, 1986.

8. Genesis 7:24; 8:3,4, etc. In Revelation, 42 months = 3 1/2 years = 1260 days, etc. We are indebted to Sir Robert Anderson's classic, *The Coming Prince*, originally published in 1894, for this insight.

9. Nehemiah 2:5-8, 17, 18. There were three other decrees, but they were concerned with the rebuilding of the Temple, not the cityand the walls: Cyrus, 537 B.C., Ezra 1:2-4; Darius, Ezra 6:1-5, 8, 12; Artaxerxes, 458 B.C. Ezra 7:11-26.

10. The English Bible translates *Nagid* as "prince." However, it should be "king." *Nagid* is first used of King Saul.

11. John 6:15; 7:30, 44; etc.

12. Recorded in all 4 Gospels: Matthew 21:1-9; Mark 11:1-10; Luke 19:29-39; John 12:12-16.

13. The Hallel Psalm 118: note verse 26.

14. This was the day that passover lambs were being presented for acceptability. Four days later, Jesus would be offered as our Passover.

15. Luke 3:1: Tiberius appointed, 14 A.D.; + 15th year = 29 A.D.. 4th Passover, 32 A.D. (April 6).

16. Luke 19:41-44.

17.   Leviticus 7:20; Psalm 37:9; Proverbs 2:22; Isaiah 53:7-9.

18.   Interval also implied: Daniel 9:26; Isaiah 61:1, 2 (Re: Luke 4:18-20); Revelation 12:5, 6. Also: Isaiah 54:7; Hosea 3:4, 5; Amos 9:10, 11; (Acts 15:13-18); Micah 5:2, 3; Zechariah 9:9, 10; Luke 1:31,3 2; 21:24.

19.   Luke 19:42 until Romans 11:25.

20.   Matthew 13:34, 35; Ephesians 3:5, 9.

21.   There are briefing packages available on *The Coming World Leader*, and *The New World Order,* from Koinonia House.

22.   This is the "Covenant with Hell," Isaiah 28:15; Zechariah 11:15-17 et al.

23.   Daniel 12:7.

24.   Revelation 11:2; 13:5.

25.   Revelation 11:3; Daniel 12:6.

26.   Daniel 9:27.

27.   Daniel 7:25; 4:16, 23, 25.

28.   Matthew 24:15.

29.   An "abomination" in the Bible is idol worship. The "abomination of desolation" is the ultimate insult possible: erecting an idol in the most sacred spot on the Planet Earth: in the Holy of Holies of the Temple in Jerusalem.

30.   It is also mentioned in John 10:22.

31.   2 Thessalonians 2:4.

32.   Jesus was, in effect, quoting Daniel 12:1. This period is also known as the "Time of Jacob's Trouble." Cf.Isaiah 61:2; Zechariah 12, 14; Revelation 19:19; et al.

33.   We strongly urge a careful study of the Seventy Weeks. Koinonia House publishes a briefing package, *Daniel's 70 Weeks*, as well as extensive expositional commentaries (on tape, with notes) on Revelation, Daniel, and other books of the Bible.

34.   See *The Road to Holocaust*, by Hal Lindsey, Bantam Books, New York, 1989.

35.   Jesus Himself addressed this in Revelation 2:9 and again in 3:9.

36.   Eschatology is the field of theology which focuses on the "last things."

37.   Daniel 9:2 and Matt 2:6 (Micah 5:2) are just two examples.

38. Also, Emmanuel Lacunza (Ben Ezra) in 1812, Edward Irving in 1816, and Margaret McDonald in 1830.

39. The original "pre-millenial, pre-tribulational" views can be traced throughout church history. The essentials of these views appear in the *Epistle of Barnabas,* (A.D. 100) and other early writings: Irenaeus, in *Against Heresies;* Hippolytus, a disciple of Irenaeus (2nd century); and Justin Martyr, *Dialogue with Trypho.* These views also show up in *The Approaching Deliverance of the Church,* by Peter Jurieu, 1687; Philip Doddridge's *Commentary on the New Testament,* 1738; Dr. John Gill's *Commentary on the New Testament,* 1 Thessalonians 4:15-17, 1748; James Macknight's *Commentary on the Apostolical Epistles,* 1763; and Thomas Scott's *Commentary on the Holy Bible,* 1792. The recent discovery of the writings of Ephraem the Syrian also confirm this view: Thomas D. Ice and Timothy J. Demy, *Bibliothecra Sacra,* July--September 1995.

40. John 14:1-3; 1 Thessalonians 4:15-17; 1 Corinthians 15:51-53.

41. See our briefing package, *From Here to Eternity* for a complete study of this critical subject.

42. Daniel 9:27.

43. 2 Thessalonians 2:7-9. Only God has ever restrained sin.

44. Ezekiel 38:14.

45. Romans 11:25.

* * *

For a complete background on the Seventy Weeks of Daniel, we are indebted to Sir Robert Anderson's *The Coming Prince*, originally published in 1894, but now available in any Christian bookstore.

Chapter 17:

The Placement of Ezekiel 38

Study to shew thyself approved unto God, a workman that needeth not to be ashamed, rightly dividing the word of truth.

2 Timothy 2:15

O Daniel, shut up the words, and seal the book, even to the time of the end: many shall run to and fro, and knowledge shall be increased.

Daniel 12:4

One of the many controversies surrounding the Ezekiel 38 passage is its timing: when does this invasion occur with respect to the other events in the classic prophetic scenario?

Past History?

Some "liberal" scholars view the Ezekiel passage as historically fulfilled. They attempt to ascribe the passage as referring to a previous incursion which happened long ago.

At some time during the years of Scythian domination, some of them did make a lightning raid along the coast of Israel to the borders of Egypt.[1] (An incident involving the plundering of the temple of Aphrodite is ascribed by Herodotus as the origin of "the female sickness" [venereal disease?] as "punishment.")[2] At Tell Defenneh (Tahpanhes) in Egypt, hundreds of characteristic two-edged, trilobate, and pyramidal bronze arrowheads were found together with an iron dagger of a Scythian type, again, corroborating the Herodotus account.[3]

Beth Shean

According to the Byzantine chroniclers, Eusebius and Syncellus, one result of the Scythian incursion into Israel was the renaming of Beth Shean, south of the Sea of Galilee, as Scythopolis.[4] Several objects from Beth Shean have been found: a terra-cotta figure in a Scythian costume[5] and a curse tablet bearing so-called Scythian names.[6]

The earliest reference to the name Scythopolis occurs in Polybius (2nd century B.C.). The Septuagint[7] calls Beth Shean "a city of Scythians,"[8] and this implies that it carried this name even before Israel conquered Canaan. Some scholars, however, believe that the city carried the name later as the friends and allies of Hellenistic Egypt.[9]

The remarkable excavations recently undertaken at Beth Shean has revealed one of the largest ancient Roman discoveries and many more finds are likely. It is interesting that this extensive excavation was undertaken, in part, to provide work for the recent influx of Russian immigrants. There is an interesting irony that the descendants of the Scythians are the very ones who are now revealing their own colorful history by working at the dig.[10]

The scope of the Ezekiel passage--and its subsequent events--clearly goes beyond any previous historical event. The passage is clearly directed at the "latter days" and is intimately connected with the events which climax in the "Day of the Lord" and the Second Coming.[11]

After the Millennium?

There is a reference in Revelation 20:8 that mentions Gog and Magog instigating a rebellion *after* the Millennium, that causes some commentators to attempt to apply this to the Ezekiel passage. However, the language in Ezekiel clearly indicates that the battle described *anticipates*, rather than follows, the coming of the Israel's Messiah and the establishment of the Millennial kingdom.

(The reappearance of Gog and Magog at the close of the Millennium was reviewed in chapter 15.)

Armageddon Sequence?

The traditional, and well supported, view is that this battle is associated with the sequence of events which climax in the judgement at Armageddon. This view would integrate the events of Ezekiel 38 and 39 with the sequence of events detailed in Daniel 11, and thus equate Gog and Magog with Daniel's King of the North.

The emphasis on the judgement of God also supports this view.[12]

> *Thou shalt falls upon the mountains of Israel, thou, and all thy bands, and the person that is with thee: I will give thee unto the ravenous birds of every sort, and to the beasts of the field to be devoured.*
> *Thou shalt fall upon the open field: for I have spoken it, saith the Lord GOD.*
>
> Ezekiel 39:4-5

This language is very similar to Revelation 19:17-18 and causes many commentators to link the passages. Clearly, the description of the judgement is consistent with placing the Ezekiel invasion with the climax of the events of the "Day of the Lord."

Another indication is the emphasis that Israel is, prior to the incursion, dwelling safely.[13] Some infer this safety is the result of a peace treaty with the Coming World Leader (which he abrogates in the middle of the seven year period known as the 70th Week of Daniel.)[14]

This view is the most commonly held view among conservative prophetic authorities. It is this view that was also summarized in the classic, *The Late Great Planet Earth*, the best seller that resulted in the New York Times awarding Hal Lindsey "The Author of the Decade" for nonfiction in 1980.

The Completion of the Church

Paul revealed that Israel's "blindness" is to endure until the Church is completed[15] and then God will once again deal with the world *through Israel*. Ezekiel 39:22-25 focuses on this, and, therefore, the Church interval has been completed.

> *So the house of Israel shall know that I am the LORD their God from that day and forward.*
>
> *And the heathen shall know that the house of Israel went into captivity for their iniquity: because they trespassed against me, therefore hid I my face from them, and gave them into the hand of their enemies: so fell they all by the sword.*

> *According to their uncleanness and according to*
> *their transgressions have I done unto them, and hid*
> *my face from them.*
>
> *Therefore thus saith the Lord GOD; Now will I*
> *bring again the captivity of Jacob, and have mercy*
> *upon the whole house of Israel, and will be jealous*
> *for my holy name;*
>
> *Ezekiel 39:22-25*

The final verses of the Ezekiel 39 recap the whole passage, emphasizing that God is once again dealing with His people Israel.

Invasion Precedes the 70th Week?

The classic, and well defended, placement of the Ezekiel 38 event is at the end of the 70th Week of Daniel.[16] It is the key event that highlights that God is dealing, once again, with Israel nationally.

However, there are also some of us who believe that the Ezekiel 38 event *precedes*, and perhaps leads to, or sets the stage for, the events during 70th Week of Daniel.[17] This view attempts to reconcile the absence of mention of Egypt, Babylon, and the Coming World Leader (the "Antichrist") which are so prominent in the other passages concerning the "70th Week," and yet are conspicuously absent in the Ezekiel 38 passage. Furthermore, technicalities in the analysis of Daniel 11 also seem to present problems to some, in considering Ezekiel 38 as a parallel passage.

To some of us, the nuclear catastrophe indicated in Ezekiel 38 and 39 may well set the stage for the global supervision and the covenant which lead to the "70th Week" and its attendant climax.

The Rapture of the Church

The Bible describes an astonishing event which clearly precedes the "70th Week of Daniel": the snatching away (Greek, *harpazo;* Latin, *rapturo*) of the Church.[18] While not free of controversy, the critical insight that most conservative scholars agree on is that the Church *does not* witness the Ezekiel 38 invasion from the Earth: that the "rapture" of the Church *precedes* these events.

If this is the case, the apparent proximity of the Magog invasion of Israel has profound implications for all of us!

The author of this book is in an unusual position. I believe that Ezekiel 38 could happen at any time. But if the rapture happens first, that must mean it is very close, indeed. For example, if you are driving down your main street, and you notice that the stores are decorating for Christmas--you know Thanksgiving is not far away!

But the biggest issue is yet to be addressed...

Endnotes:

1.   Herodotus 1.105.

2.   F. Wilke, "Das Skythenproblem im Jeremiabuch," in *Alttestamentliche Studien fur R. Kittle,* J. C. Hinrichs, Leipzig, 1913, pp. 228-229.

3.   Sulimirski, "Scythian Antiquities," p. 305.

4.   *Ibid.,* p. 294.

5.   F. M. Abel, "Melanges," *Revue biblique,* 9, 1912, pp 409-423.

6.   H. C. Youtie and Campbell Bonner, "Two Curse Tablets from Beisan,", *Transactions and Proceedings of the American Philolgical Association,* 68, 1937, p. 43-77.

7.   Judges 1:27.

8.   Cf. Judith 3:10; II Maccabees 12:29; Pliny the Elder, *Natural History,* 5.16.

9.   M. Avi-Yonah, "Scythopolis," *Israel Exploration Journal,* 12, 1962, p. 127.

10. No Scythian remains were found earlier by the University of Pennsylvania excavations at Beth Shean since their work concentrated on the imposing tell. The later city of Scythopolis was discovered on the plain below the tell. Scythopolis lay beyond the scope of the Museum excavation. F. W. James, "Beth-Shan," *Expedition,* 3, 1961, p. 35-36.

11. Ezekiel 38:8, 16.

12. Ezekiel 39:17-21 continues the grim passage by describing the strange feast alluded to in verse 4, and that also seems to link with Revelation 19:17-18.

13. Ezekiel 38:8, 11, 14; 39:26.

14. Daniel 9:27. A clear understanding of the last four verses of Daniel 9 is the eseential foundation to any serious study of Bible prophecy. See *Daniel's 70 Weeks,* Koinonia House.

15. Romans 11:25.

16. Hal Lindsey, *The Late Great Planet Earth,* is the famous classic that supports this view.

17. Chuck Smith, Grant Jeffery, and Chuck Missler are among those who consider this alternative a clear possibility.

18. I Corinthians 15:51-53; I Thessalonians 4:13-17.

Chapter 18:

The
Ultimate Issue

The prudent see danger and take refuge,
But the simple keep going and suffer for it.

Proverbs 27:12

For I know the plans I have for you, declares the Lord,
plans to prosper you and not to harm you, plans to give you
hope and a future.

Jeremiah 29:11

The prospects of a nuclear confrontation in the Middle East are terrifying, and the global upheaval which would inevitably ensue is too easily dismissed as simply unthinkable. Already the anticipation and preparations are beginning to impact our lives. Not a day goes by without some incident of international terrorism, another interdiction of smuggled nuclear material into a Muslim country, or evidence of increasing tensions over the struggle over Jerusalem.

However, the real issue that the impending Magog invasion brings onto our own horizon goes far beyond the conflict in the Middle East. The broader implications must preempt all of our personal priorities.

The astonishing realization for each of us is that *all* of the elements of the classic Biblical scenario are closing in for the final culmination of mankind's rule on the Planet Earth.

This review has highlighted the reasons why the famous battle of Ezekiel 38 now appears on the horizon. But this is only one element of many. There are, in addition, a series of parallel themes that comprise the tide of events that ultimately lead to the famed climax of Armageddon. The emergent reality is that *every major theme of Bible prophecy is visibly moving toward the climax.*

This isn't a question of some "pet theory" about some specific verse or passage. It is conspicuously obvious by simply comparing the trends in world events with the specific details specified in the Biblical passages.

The incredible realization is that you and I are being plunged into a period of time about which the Bible says more than it does about any other period of history--including the time that Jesus walked the shores of Galilee or climbed the mountains of Judea!

It isn't just a question of Ezekiel 38 and the impending tensions in the Middle East. There are the similar positionings observable on the rest of the global horizon.

Europe

Daniel chapters 2 and 7 clearly present an overview of all of Gentile history in advance. After the Babylonian, Persian, and Greek empires, Rome would arise to power, but in two phases. The first is well known; the final phase is on the horizon. The final form of this world empire will once again control the economic, political, and religious destinies on the Planet Earth.

With the 12 nations of the European Union now being joined by the seven nations of the European Free Trade Association, and others, there is now a total of more than 23 nations confederating, with a combined population of more than twice that of the United States.

(The Maastricht Treaty has obsoleted the Treaty of Rome and provides for a unified European superstate with a common foreign policy, common military, and, ultimately, a common currency. It is regarded by the experts as the most significant political event of the century, and most Americans are not even aware of its existence.)

This power bloc is filling the void left by the breakup of the Soviet Union and the decline of the United States.[1]

Babylon

Isaiah 13 and 14, Jeremiah 50 and 51, and Revelation 17 and 18, all describe the destruction of the city of Babylon. Many commentators confuse the *Fall* of Babylon in 539 B.C. with the *Destruction* of Babylon, yet future, as described in the Bible. Babylon has yet to be destroyed as the prophets predicted. It will be. Precisely as they have written.

Saddam Hussein has spent more than 20 years rebuilding the city of Babylon, and its re-emergence is yet another one of the major events of Bible prophecy.[2]

Israel

There have been alarmists throughout history that have felt--for one reason or another--that "the end was near." But all one had to do was consider the State of Israel. Numerous prophecies clearly require the reestablishment of Israel in the land. The Bible indicates that when they are regathered into their land the *second* time--the first regathering was after the Babylonian captivity in the 6th century B.C.--Israel would never again be uprooted.[3] The dramatic regathering of the Jews to their long-promised homeland in recent years is one of the most amazing miracles--and irrefutable testimonies--in itself.

It has happened exactly as God said it would.

Jerusalem

Zechariah pointed out that everyone who burdens themselves with Jerusalem would be destined to frustration. It would be a "cup of trembling"; a "burdensome stone."[4] It would be the unsolvable dilemma for all the nations of the world.

That is manifestly absurd. Here is a city with no natural resources, not even a harbor; no reason to be internationally significant. Yet there it is.

As you read this book, the late lights are burning in every nation's capital, pondering what to do about the continuing tensions over Jerusalem. Every country in the international arena is perplexed as to what posture to take concerning this fabled city.[5]

The Bible predicted that Israel would regain control of Biblical Jerusalem. On June 7, 1967, it happened exactly as God said it would.

The Coming Temple

The Bible also predicted--three times in the New Testament alone--that the Temple would be rebuilt as part of the final scenario.[6]

The astonishing thing is that the preparations have begun. There are more than 200 young men in *yeshivas*--rabbinical schools--presently in training to serve as priests in the anticipated Temple. (You probably realize, of course, that one cannot be a priest without Levi genes!)

The Temple Institute has completed more than 63 of the 103 implements required for service in the Temple. If you visit Jerusalem, you can examine the silver trumpets, the gold headdress and jeweled breastplate of the High Priest, the lottery boxes for selecting the scapegoat, and other items actually being prepared for service in the anticipated Temple.[7]

Computerized looms are weaving the priestly vestments. Scientists are scanning the world for the correct marine snails to yield the Levitical blue and the royal purple dyes.

Engineers and technicians are exploiting ground penetrating radar, infrared photography, and other advanced technologies in an effort to confirm just precisely where the original Temples stood.

(When I was doing some research at the Temple Institute, I discovered an electrical wiring diagram for the coming Temple. I mentioned to Rabbi Chaim Richman, my host, my surprise, "You are going to all this trouble to be faithful to the

Tenach, the Mishnah, the Tosefta, and other sources--and you have an electrical wiring diagram?"

"Chuck," he said, "You need to understand, where the ancient sources speak, we follow them carefully. But where they are silent, we feel free to exploit any technology available. You see, we are building a Temple for the future, not the past."

I responded, "Then you are going to have facilities for television?" He was puzzled by my presumption.

I explained, "Jesus predicted you will have. In Matthew 24:15, He describes an event, within the Holy of Holies, that everyone in Judea is to be *watching* for. Only the high priest, and only on *Yom Kippur*, is alowed in that sanctified space. How can everyone in Judea see it? On CNN, of course!"

He wasn't as amused as I was.

Access to the Temple Mount site is, at present, controlled by WAQF, the high Muslim coucil. The political tensions are increasing and speculations are intensifying. But in the near future, a window of opportunity will open and the actual Temple rebuilding will begin.[8] Watch for it.

The Ultimate Issue

The real issue is, of course, not Magog. Nor Europe. Not Babylon. Not Israel, nor Jerusalem, nor the Temple.

The real issue is Jesus Christ.

Was He *really* who He said He was? Is He really about to *return* to intervene in the history of mankind on the Planet Earth?

If so, how does all this affect *you?* What is your position with respect to Jesus Christ?

Don't gamble your eternity that the Bible is wrong.

This has nothing to do with "religion." It is entirely involved with your *personal relationship* with Him. This may sound trite, or hackneyed, but your eternity depends on this, and on this alone.

God has a destiny for you that is so fantastic that there is nothing you can possibly do to *earn* it. The "good news" is that it is available simply for the asking.

If you haven't dealt with this issue seriously, this eclipses everything else in your life. Deal with it *now.*

Make an unequivocal, personal commitment to Him, in prayer, in the privacy of your own will, right now. And then share it with someone you trust spiritually.

It is unquestionably the most important decision of your life.

The Grand Adventure

You may have already dealt with this issue. What then?

We strongly urge you to take the Bible *seriously.* Find out for yourself what the Bible says about the "last days." Find out for yourself what the Bible says about Russia, about Europe, about Babylon, about Israel, about Jerusalem, and the Temple.

Don't take our word for it. It's too important.

It's now time to do *your own* homework. The urgency of these issues should impact your personal priorities. Make a renewed commitment to dig in and find out for yourself what is on the prophetic horizon, and how you can be a participant, and not just a spectator, in God's Grand Adventure as it unfolds before us![9]

Free Gift:

We publish an intelligence journal, Personal UPDATE--32 pages every month--in an attempt to highlight the Biblical relevance of current events. It is normally $20.00/year; however, there should be a gift certificate in this book for a full year's free introductory subscription. If it is missing, just call or write us. We will be glad to register you for an initial year as our way of getting better acquainted and in the hopes that you will find it worth renewing.

Keep in touch: **1 (800) KHOUSE1**

or write:

Chuck Missler
c/o Koinonia House
P. O. Box D
Coeur d'Alene ID 83816

or if you're "net literate"--

email: update@khouse.org
Internet Web Site: http://www.khouse.org/khouse

Endnotes:

1. For a complete review of the European suprastate and its Biblical implications, see *Iron Mixed With Clay*, Koinonia House.

2. The author has available as briefing package on *The Mystery of Babylon* which includes a comprehensive background and update on this prophetic fulfillment.

3. Isaiah 11:11f.

4. Zechariah 12.

5. One of the best treatments on this timely subject is *A Cup of Trembling*, by Dave Hunt, Harvest House, 1995.

6. Matthew 24:15; II Thessalonians 2:4; Revelation 11:1,2.

7. The Temple Institute, 24 Misgav Ladach St., Jewish Quarter, Old City, Jerusalem, Israel.

8. See *The Coming Temple, Center Stage for the Final Countdown,* by Chuck Missler and Don Stewart.

9. There are two basic briefing package which might prove useful: *A Walk Thru the Bible,* a strategic review of both the Old and New Testaments on two tape cassettes, with study notes; and *How to Study the Bible*, which summarizes the author's own experiences and helpful hints from his own experience. Available at your bookstore or from Koinonia House.

Bibliography

Extensive source references have been included to permit further study. Where sources are no longer in print, primary citations and references have been carried forward into the notes.

Albright, F.W., *Yahweh and the Gods of Canaan*, Doubleday, Garden City NJ, 1968

Alders, J. G., *Gog en Magog in Ezechiel*, J. H Kok, Kamapen, 1951;

Alexander, Ralph, *Ezekiel*, Moody Press, Chicago, Ill.,1976.

Artamonov, M.I., *Treasures from Scythian Tombs in the Hermitage Museum*, Thames and Hudson, London, 1969.

Artamonov, M.I., *The Splendor of Scythian Art: Treasures from the Scythian Tombs*, Praeger, NY, 1969; idem. *Treasures from the Scythian Tombs in the Hermitage Museum*, Thames and Hudson, London, 1969.

Barnett, R.D., *Phrygia and the Peoples of Anatolia in the Iron Age*, Cambridge University, Cambridge, 1967;

Beregovaia, N.A., et al. *Contributions to the Archaeology of the Soviet Union*, AMS Press, New York, 1966.

Blaiklock, E.M., *Zondervan Pictorial Bible Atlas*, Zondervan, Grand Rapids, 1969, p. 45;

Boardsman, John, *The Greeks Overseas*, 2nd ed., Thames and Hudson, London, 1980.

Bruce, F.F., *Commentary on...Colossians*, Eerdmans, Grand Rapids, 1957,

Bryce, T.R., "Phrygia and Lydia," *Encyclopedia of Ancient Civilizations*, A. Cotterell, ed., Mayflower, NY, 1980,

Clancy, Tom, *The Hunt for Red October*, U.S. Naval Institute, 1985.

Bruce Cohen, *Israel, Arabs and the Middle East*, Har Tavor Publsihing Ltd, Wynnewood PA, 1991.

Colson, F.H., Whitaker, G.H. and Marcus, Ralph, *Philo*, Loeb Classical Library, London, 1929-1953.

Cook, M.J., *The Greeks in Ionia and the East*, Praeger, New York, 1963;

Culican, W., *The Medes and Persians*, Praeger, New York, 1965,

Custance, A.C., *Noah's Three Sons*, Zondervan, Grand Rapids, 1975,

Davis, J.J., *Paradise to Prison*, Baker, Grand Rapids, 1975,

Dhorme, E., "Les peuples issus de Japhet d'apres le chapitre X de la Genese," *Recueil Edouard dhorme*, Imprimerie Nationale, Paris, 1951

Dunbabin, T.J., *The Greeks and Their Eastern Neighbours*, Society for the Promotion of Hellenic Studies, London, 1959;

Edwards, E.S., et al, ed., *Cambridge Ancient History*, 1975,

Eichrodt, Walther, *Ezekiel*, Westminster Press, Philadelphia, PA, 1970.

Ellison, H.L., "Gog and Magog," *Illustrated Bible Dictionary*, Ed. N. Hillyer, Inter-Varsity, Leicester, 1980

Encyclopedia of Religion and Ethics, ed. James Hastings, T & T Clark, Edinburgh, 1908,

Encyclopedia of Religion, eds. Paul Meagher, Thomas O'Brien, Consuela Aherne, Corpus Pubilsihers, Washington DC, 1979.

Encyclopedia Britannica

Encyclopedia of Islam, E.J. Prill, Leiden, 1913, I:302; I:406; III:1093

Fairbbairn, Patrick, *Commentary on Ezekiel*, Zondervan, Grand Rapids, Michigan, 1960.

Feinberg, Charles Lee, *The Prophecy of Ezekiel*, Moody Press, Chicago, Ill., 1969.

Fuller, J.F.C., *The Generalship of Alexander the Great*, Rutgers University, New Brunswick NJ, 1960,

Georgacas, D., *The Names for the Asia Minor Peninsula*, Carl Winter, Heidelberg, 1971.

Gesenius, Wilhelm, *A Hebrew and English Lexicon of the Old Testament*, Crocker and Brewster, Boston, 1872

Ghirshman, R., "Invasion des nomades," *Dark Ages and Nomads, c. 1000 B.C.*, ed.

Ghirshman, R., *The Art of Ancient Iran*, Golden Press, NY, 1964,

Ghrishman, R., *Tombe Princiere de Ziwiye et le debut de l'art animalier scythe,* La Societe Iranienne pour la Conversation due Patrimoine National, Paris, 1979,

Gimbutas, M., *Prehistory of Eastern Europe,* Peabody Museum, Cambridge MA, 1956,

Gingrich, F.W. and Danker, Frederick, *A Greek-English Lexicon of the New Testament and other Early Christian Literature,* University of Chicago Press, Chicago and London, 1957.

Grakov, B.N., *Die Skythen,* Deutscher Verlag der Wissenschaften, Berlin, 1980,

Grayson, A.K., *Assyrian Royal Inscriptions,* O. Harrassowitz, Wiesbaden, 1976, vol 2,

Gryaznov, M. P., *The Ancient Civilization of Southern Siberia,* Crowles, New York, 1969.

Hatch, Edwin, and Redpath, Henery A., *Concordance to the Septuagint and the Other Greek Versions of the Old Testament,* Akademische Druck-U-Verlagsanstalt, Graz, Austria,, 2 vols., 1954 (1897).

Hitchcock, Mark, *After the Empire,* Tyndale House, Wheaton IL, 1994.

How, W.W., and Wells, J., *A Commentary on Herodotus,* Clarendon, Oxford, 1961

Hunt, Dave, *A Woman Rides the Beast,* Harvest House, Eugene OR, 1995.

Hunt, Dave, *A Cup of Trembling,* Harvest House, Eugene OR, 1994.

Ironside, Henry A., *Ezekiel,* Loizeaux Bros., Neptune, N.J., 1949.

Jefferies, Grant, *The Final Warning,* Frontier Research Books, Toronto, Canada, 1995.

Jones, Tom, *Paths to the Ancient Past,* Free Press, NY, 1967

Kathir, Ibn , *The Signs before the Day of Judgement,* Dar Al Taqwa Ltd, London, 1992. (Ismail Abul-Fadl Umar Ibn Kathir was one of the leading scholars of Islam of the 14th century. Excerpted from his 14 volume history of Islam.)

Keil, C.F., and Delitzsch, F., *Biblical Commentary on the Prophecies of Ezekiel,* T. and T. Clark, Edinburgh, 1891, vol 2

Kent, R.G., *Old Persian,* 2nd ed., American Oriental Society, New Haven CT, 1953, p.

Kesses HaSofer, *Bereishis - Genesis,* A New Translatioon with a Commentary Anthologised from Talmudic, Midrashic and Rabbinic Sources, Mesorah Publications, Lt.

Knockblock, E., *Beyond the Oxus: Archaeology, Art and Architecture of Central Asia,* Rowman and Littlefield, Totowa NJ, 1972.

Legrand, E. "De la 'malignite d'Herodote," *Melanges Gustav Glotz,* Presses Universitaires de France, Paris, 1932

Levine, L.D., *Two Neo-Assyrian Stelae from Iran,* Royal Ontario Museum, Toronto, 1972,

Lightfoot, J.B., *Commentary on Saint Paul's Epistles to the Colossians and Philemon,* Zondervan, 1957 (reprint of 1879 edition),

Lindsey, Hal, *The Late Great Planet Earth,* Bantam Books, NY

Lindsey, Hal, *The Final Battle,* Western Front Ltd, Palos Verdes CA, 1995.

Lindsey, Hal, *The Road to Holocaust,* Bantam Books, NY, 1989.

Lorimer, H.L., *Homer and the Monuments,* Macmillan, London, 1950,

Luckenbill, D.D., ed. *Ancient Records of Assyria and Babylonia,* Univesity of Chicago, Chicago, 1927, vol 2

Malachi Martin, *The Keys of This Blood,* Simon Schuster, New York NY 1990.

Masson V.M., and Saianidi, V.I., *Central Asia: Turkmenia Before the Achaemenids,* Thames and Hudson, London, 1972,

McGovern, W.M., *The Early Empires of Central Asia,* University of North Carolina, Chapel Hill, 1939,

Miller, David, *Submarines of the World,* Salamander Books, London, 1991.

Miller, William McElwee, *A Christian's Response to Islam,* Presbyterian and Reformed Publishing Co., Phillipsburg, NJ, 1979.

Moore, John, *Jane's Fighting Ships of the 20th Century,* Mallard Press, New York, 1991.

Morey, Robert, *The Islamic Invasion,* Harvest House. Eugene OR. Lucid, well documented, an excellent reference.

Musk, Bill, *The Unseen Face of Islam,* Monarch Publications Ltd, London, 1989.

Naster, P., *L'Asie Mineure et l'Assyrie,* Bureaux du Museon, Louvain, 1938;

National Museum of Ukranian History, 1993 *Golden Warriors of the Ukranian Steppes,* (Chaykovskiy, S.M.; Khardayev, V.M.; Belan, Yu.A.; Berezovaya, S.A.; Klochko, L.S.; Koreskaya, S.A.; Shamina, T.F.; Stelets, Degtyareva, M.S.; T.G.; Arustamyan, Zh.g.; Garbuz, B.B. (trans. from Russian text, Caroline Horne, Geoffrey H. Harper.)

Olmstead, A.T., "The Assyrians in Asia Minor," in *Anatolian Studies,* ed. W. H. Buckler, Manchester University, Manchester, 1923; idem, *History of Assyria,* University of Chicago, Chicago, 1923

Olmstead, A.T., *History of Assyria,* 2nd ed., University of Chicago, Chicago, 1951,

Page, D.I., *History and the Homeric Iliad,* Univesity of California, Berkely, 1959,

Parpola, S., *Neo-Assyrian Toponyms,* Butzon and Bercker, Kevelaer, West Germany, 1970

Payne, J.B., *Enclyopedia of Bible Prophecy, the Complete Guide to Scriptural Predictions and Their Fulfillment,* Harper and Row, NY, 1973,

Peters, Joan, *From Time Immemorial: The Origins of the Arab-Jewish Conflict Over Palestine,* Michael Joseph, London, 1984.. An essential and comprehensive documentation of the real truth behind the Palestinian myths driving foreign policy today.

Phillips, E.D., *The Royal Hordes: Nomad Peoples of the Steppes,* McGraw-Hill, New York, 1965,

Piotrovsky, Dr. Boris ,*From the Lands of the Scythians,* Metropolitan Museum of Art Bulletin, Vol XXXII, No. 5, 1974.

Piotrovsky, Dr. Boris, *The Ancient Civilization of Urartu,* Cowles, NY, 1969,

Potratz, J., *Die Skythen in Sudrussland,* Raggi, Basel, 1963.

Preston, Anthony, *Submarines,* Bison Books, London, 1985.

Rahlfs, Alfred, ed.*Jd Est Vetus Testamentum Graece IVXTA LXX Interpretes,* Vol 2., Privileg, Wurtt, Bibelanstalt, Stuttgart, 1935;

Ravn, O.E., *Herodotus' Description of Babylon,* A. Busck, Copenhagen, 1942;

Rice, R., *The Scythians,* 3rd ed., Praeger, New York, 1961

Rices, T., *Scythians,* Советская Археология, no. 2, 1959,

Bibliography

Rudenko, S.I., *Frozen Tombs of Siberia: The Pazyryk Burials of Iron-Age Horsemen,* University of California, Berkeley, 1970.

Rybakov, B.A., Геродотова Скифия, (Herodotus's Scythia), Nauka, Moscow, 1979,

Ryrie, C.C., *The Ryrie Study Bible,* Moody, Chicago, 1978

Scofield, C. I., ed., *The New Scofield Reference Bible*, English, E.S., 1967

Scofield, C.I., ed., *The Scofield Reference Bible,* Oxford University, 1917

Selincourt, A. de *The World of Herodotus,* Little, Brown, Boston, 1962

Sherwin-White, A.N., *Racial Prejudice in Imperial Rome,* Cambridge University, Cambridge, 1967;

Snodgrass, A.M., *Arms and Armour of the Greeks,* Thames and Hudson, London, 1967,

Snowden, F.M., *Blacks in Antiquity,* Harvard University, Cambridge MA, 1970;

Spiegelberg, W., *The Credibility of Herodotus' Account of Egypt in the Light of the Egyptian Monuments,* Blackwell, Oxford, 1927;

Sulimirski, T., *Prehistoric Russia,* Humanities Press, New York, 1970;

Sulimirski, T., *The Sarmatians,* Thames and Hudson, London, 1970.

Taylor, John B., *Ezekiel,* Tyndale Old Testament Commentaries, Inter-Varsity Press, Downers Grove, Ill., 1969.

Thomposon, R.C., *The Prisms of Esarhaddon and Ashurbanipal,* British Museum, London, 191,

Tretiakov P.N., and Mongait, A.L., eds., *Contributions to the Ancient History of the USSR,* Peabody Museum, Cambridge MA, 1961,

U. S. Government, *Operator's Manual for Marking Set, Contamination: Nuclear, Biological, Chemical,* TM 3-9905-001-10, Department of the Army, 1982.

U. S. Government, *Soviet Military Power,* Department of Defense, U. S. Government

Vaughn, C., "Colossians," in *The Expositor's Bible Commentary,* ed. F. E. Gaebelein, Zondervan, Grand Rapids MI, 1978, vol 11,

Vos, M.F., *Scythian Archers,* J. B. Wolters, Goningen, 1963,

Weippert, M., "Menahem von Israel und seine Zeitgenossen in einer Steleninschrift des assyrischen Konigs Tiglath-pileser III. us dem Iran", *Zeitschrift des Deutschen Palastina-Vereins* 89, 1973, 30.

Wevers, John W., *Ezekiel,* The New Century Bible Commentary, Wm. B. Eerdmans, Grand Rapids, Michigan, 1969.

Wilke, F., "Das Skythenproblem im Jeremiabuch," in *Alttestamentliche Studien fur R. Kittle,* J. C. Hinrichs, Leipzig, 1913,

Yadin, Y., *The Art of Warfare in Biblical Lands,* Weidenfeld and Nicolson, London, 1963,

Yamauchi, Edwin M., *Foes from the Northern Frontier,* Baker Book House, Grand Rapids, Michigan, 1982

Yamauchi, Edwin W., *Persia and the Bible*, Baker Book House, Grand Rapids MI 1990

Ye'or, Bat, *The Dhimmi: Jews and Christians under Islam,* Associated University Presses, Cranbury, 1985; *Les Chretiente D'Orient Entre Jihad et Dhimmitude,* Les Editions du Cerf, Paris, 1991.

Young, R.W., *Gordion,* Archaeological Museum of Ankara, 1968,

Young, R.S., "The Nomadic Impact: Gordion," *Dark Ages and Nomads c. 1000 BC,* ed. M.J. Melink, Nederlands Histoisch-Archaeologisch Instituut, Istanbul, 1964,

Youssef Michael, *America, Oil, and the Islamic Mind,* Zonbdervan Publishing House, Grand Rapids, MI, 1983, 1991.

Zimmerli, Walther, *Ezekiel,* 2 Vols., Fortress Press, Philadelphia, PA, 1983.

Большая Советская Энциклопедия, *Great Soviet Encylopedia,* 3rd ed., 1979,

Journals and Periodicals

American Journal of Semitic Languages
American Anthropologist
American Journal of Archaelogy
Annali Istituto Orientale di Napoli
Annals of Archaeology and Anthropology
Antike Welt
Archaeologiai Ertesito
Archaeology
Artibus Asiae
Bulletin of the Institute of Archaeology
Classical Journal
Das Altertum
Dumbarton Oaks Papers
Expedition
Historia
Iraq
Israel Exploration Journal
Journal of Biblical Literature
Journal of Hellenic Studies
Journal of the Evangelical Theological Society
Journal of the American Oriental Society
Journal of Semitic Studies
Journal Asiatique
Journal of Near Eastern Studies
Klio
Orientalistische Literaturzeitung
Quarterly Statement, Palestine Exploration Fund
Revue de l'Universite de Bruxelles,
Revue biblique
Revue International d'Histoire Militaire
Revue anthropologique
Saeculum
Scientific American
Sumer
The Russian Review
Transactions and Proceedings of the American Philolgical Association
U.S. Naval Institute Proceedings
Советская Археология, (Sovetskaia Arkheologiia)

Subject Index

About the Author

Chuck Missler has served as a member on the Board of Directors of over a dozen public corporations, and was Chairman and Chief Executive Officer of six of them. (Four of them were key contractors to the Department of Defense and the intelligence community.)

Mr. Missler has organized major joint ventures in high technology undertakings in Russia, Central Asia, North Africa, Europe and the Middle East. As a management consultant to major corporations for strategic projects in advanced technologies, computer and communications facilities, and the petroleum industry. He has participated in numerous international mergers and acquisitions, and helped establish manufacturing facilities in seven countries. He has been a strategic consultant to both the U.S. and foreign governments.

Chuck is an honor graduate of the United States Naval Academy, and holds graduate degrees in engineering and business management. He is also a recognized authority in Biblical studies and has contributed to over 50 publications in books, tapes, and videos and has daily national broadcasts in most of the United States.

Chuck Missler is also a publisher of an international intelligence newsletter. (This book includes a gift certificate for a year's subscription to this monthly 32-page publication.)

Resources Available

Koinonia House publishes Briefing Packages which include two audio tape cassettes containing live presentations by the author, and also include extensive notes, diagrams, and references for further study. Audio tapes cassettes are a proven method for quick and easy learning while driving, cleaning up the hobby room, or just relaxing with a notepad.

These packages are available in your bookstore.

The Magog Invasion

A live presentation by the author of the highlights of this book. It was the popularity of these presentations that led to it being published as a popular book.

How to Study the Bible

Chuck shares his experiences of his five decades of his love affair with the Word of God. Unorthodox, but useful and with some surprising secrets.

A Walk Thru the Bible

A brief overview of the books of the Bible, with the aim of developing a strategic grasp of the whole, and how each book fits in. Demonstrates why these 66 books, written by 40 authors over thousands of years, are an integrated message--provably from outside our time domain. Once the unity of the whole is understood, most difficulties begin to evaporate.

Daniel's 70 Weeks

The most amazing prophecy in the Bible, clearly demonstrating the supernatual mission of Jesus Christ. It also happens to contain the key to understanding Bible prophecy; Jesus Himself pointed to it in His confidential briefing of His disciples about His Second Coming (Matthew 24:15).

This in-depth study is essential to any serious interest in end-time prophecy study.

Iron Mixed With Clay

A detailed study of Daniel 2 and 7, and their implications for today. These passages provide an overview of all of Gentile history, and the climax that is emerging on the near horizon. Includes a review of the emergent European Superstate, and the implications of the Maastricht Treaty.

Travelling with Ambassador Bill Middendorf, Chuck met with over 50 of the top leadership in Europe and reviews the surprising implications behind current developments and their Biblical relevance.

The Mystery of Babylon

The confusion and controversies about Biblical Babylon, its reemerence in Iraq, and its role in the final climax.

From Here to Eternity

A study of the physics of immortality, and our amazing destiny after death.

This study reviews the various views of eschatology--the study of the end-times. Some surprising textual discoveries illuminate the reality of the destiny of the Church, and the implications on the near horizon.

Beyond Time and Space

A review of Einstein's Theory of Relativity--for the layman--and its implications for understanding the Bible. Some surprising insights which clarify many of the traditional Biblical paradoxes.

Beyond Perception

A review of the strange discoveries of quantum physics that have led scientists to the very boundaries of reality. These amazing insights yield a whole new respect for some of the little understood passages in the Bible.

The Sword of Allah

A briefing about the rise of Islam, its origins, its goals, and its agenda. The biggest challenge to Christianity, and the Western world, over the next few decades. Pierce the deceit and propaganda that is deceiving our world and discover what is really going on.

The Coming Temple: Update

A precis, and update, of the book, *The Coming Temple*, which reviews the present preparations and recent discoveries for the rebulding of the Temple in Jerusalem. Mentioned three times in the New Testament, by Jesus, John, and Paul, this next Temple is involved in a major event just prior to the Second Coming of Christ. And the preparations to rebuild have begun.

The Mystery of the Lost Ark

Where is it? Has it really been found?

Against a study of the Tabernacle and the forthcoming Temple, the various reports and rumors are reviewed--by the consultant to CBS for their recent prime time TV special--and the prophetic implications highlighted.

The New World Order

A review of the visible march toward a global world government, and its Biblical consequences as revealed in the Bible.

The Coming World Leader

Is he about to appear on the scene? Will he be the next Pope?   Or the Messiah of Israel? Or the 12th Imam of Islam?

Background and identity of the most attractive leader the world has ever seen, and his ultimate destiny.

The Vortex Strategy

Is the United States facing a major economic upheaval? If so, what is the best strategy for personal survival in the 1990's?

(This most popular series is now available in three volumes.)

$20.00 Value

$20.00 Value

Certificate

This certificate entitles the person below to a full year's subscription to *Personal* UPDATE, a newsletter highlighting the Biblical relevance of current events.

(New subscribers only.)

Name: _____

Address: _____

City: _____ State: _____ Zip: _____

Koinonia House, P.O. Box D, Coeur d'Alene ID 83816-0347